The
Thirteenth
Step

Frances MacDonald

BALBOA.
PRESS

A DIVISION OF HAY HOUSE

Balboa Press books may be ordered through booksellers or by contacting:

Balboa Press
A Division of Hay House
1663 Liberty Drive
Bloomington, IN 47403
www.balboapress.com
1-(877) 407-4847

Because of the dynamic nature of the Internet, any web addresses or links contained in this book may have changed since publication and may no longer be valid. The views expressed in this work are solely those of the author and do not necessarily reflect the views of the publisher, and the publisher hereby disclaims any responsibility for them.

The author of this book does not dispense medical advice or prescribe the use of any technique as a form of treatment for physical, emotional, or medical problems without the advice of a physician, either directly or indirectly. The intent of the author is only to offer information of a general nature to help you in your quest for emotional and spiritual well-being. In the event you use any of the information in this book for yourself, which is your constitutional right, the author and the publisher assume no responsibility for your actions.

Any people depicted in stock imagery provided by Thinkstock are models, and such images are being used for illustrative purposes only.
Certain stock imagery © Thinkstock.

Printed in the United States of America

ISBN: 978-1-4525-6898-0 (sc)
ISBN: 978-1-4525-6899-7 (e)

Balboa Press rev. date: 2/20/2013

Table of Contents

Introduction

"In this world I live in, I can't find no way out. And I am tired of living in this world I live in. I've got everybody's number but no one to call. In fact, I just can't remember anything at all......No, they won't let me leave now, from this place where I can't pretend and I am getting older and its getting colder." *Never Really Did* - The Broken Lyre 2012 (music group)

"*To them, their alcoholic life seems the only normal one. They are restless, irritable and discontented unless they can again experience the sense of ease and comfort which comes at once by taking a few drinks – drinks which they see others taking with impunity. After they have succumbed in the desire again, as so many do, and the phenomenon of craving develops, they pass through the well-known stages of a spree, emerging remorseful with a firm resolution not to drink again. This is repeated over and over and unless this person can experience an entire psychic change there is very little hope of his recovery.*"

Alcoholics Anonymous – The Doctor's Opinion page xxix

"Most of us have been unwilling to admit we were alcoholics. No person likes to think he is bodily and mentally different from his fellows. Therefore, it is not surprising that our drinking careers have been characterized by countless vain attempts to prove we could drink like other people. The idea that somehow, someday he will control and enjoy his drinking is the great obsession of every abnormal drinker. The persistence of this illusion is astonishing. Many pursue it into the gates of insanity or death."

Alcoholics Anonymous – More About Alcoholism – page 30

Did you know the people that are the strongest are usually the most sensitive? Did you know the people who exhibit the most kindness are the first to get mistreated? Did you know the one who takes care of others all the time are usually the ones who need it the most? Did you know the 3 hardest things to say are I love you, I'm sorry, and help me? Sometimes just because a person looks happy, you have to look past their smile and see how much pain they may be in. I copied this from a friend's wall because I thought it was powerfully true. We all need to pay more attention to those around us.

What is an alcoholic? Where does alcoholism originate? Why can't we alcoholics – just stop? These questions are important and quite difficult to answer and understand. *The Broken Lyre's* lyrics above outline the recurring feeling that I went through daily. I was trapped in a world that there seemed to be no way out. Isolation, self-pity and selfish behaviour overtook my logical and analytical Virgo mind. There was nothing positive in my life to grasp. Nothing to bring me to where alcohol brought me – happy, free of problems, numb to negative situations in my life, and self-confidence. My friends and family may have reached out to help me but I was so self-centred that I didn't realize or accept their help. I definitely had an addiction to alcohol and my addictive mind was very self-absorbed.

The alcoholic does not care about anyone else. Their lives are run by an overpowering disease that does not care if it kills them.

Alcoholism does not discriminate between sex, race, wealth, health, or age. It will attack weakness, vulnerability, and spiritually weak individuals. An addiction to alcohol is not something we choose. We don't wake up one morning and say "I am so happy that I am an alcoholic." We do not choose to lose our jobs, our children, our families, our finances, our pride and reputation and our will. It happens due to a variety of things that combined together create disaster. Most alcoholics do not think or admit they have a problem until it is too late. Unfortunately awareness most often comes with a cost. It usually takes the alcoholic to *hit rock bottom* to acknowledge his/her disease. I had a problem for a very long time but it was only when I sunk to the lowest point that I finally became aware of it.

But there is hope. There is a light at the end of the tunnel. We have the control and the tools to overcome the addiction and become spiritually/divinely guided towards a connection with the universe and our Higher Power. I am not talking about the fearful God taught in Catholicism but of the inner spirit, the soul, the God-within each human being. You can call this whatever works for you. It is the fire inside, it is that knot in your stomach when you know something is not right. It is that inner voice that your ego tries to keep repressed. It is your connection to something more powerful than yourself. I choose to call it God or Higher Power. The path to this awareness is not easy and many of us stumble along the way. Our lives are controlled by our substance and we do not feel at ease without it, as stated in the AA quote above. Most often, our lives have become completely unmanageable and totally out of control. It's funny, we keep trying to convince ourselves that we are in control and we do not need others in our lives. Then the last straw occurs – we hit rock bottom – isolated, frustrated, broke, spiritually dead and close to a physical death. It is when we experience the moment that life can no longer go on this way – is the moment we start to actually 'live'. The moment we admit being *sick and tired of being sick and tired*, will our lives change.

Addiction to any substance – alcohol, drugs, gambling, and sex happens as a result of many factors combining so beautifully together. Biological factors, psychological factors, social factors, and spiritual factors. In combination, these factors create an addictive behaviour in human beings. In order to overcome addictions, one must understand the factors creating it. It is not just enough to say "I can't change - once an addict, always an addict" - not true. There are several ways of overcoming addiction. Through my personal experience, I do believe that gaining knowledge of where the addiction was created, as well as, working through a 12-step program and having a spiritual awakening are the keys to caging the addictive beast. So many people think that being abstinent from the substance or the addictive behaviour will relieve the cravings and the addiction. I wish it were that easy but the underlying issues will not go away unless they are dealt with.

In order to change your behaviour, one must change their thoughts. This does not just involve positive thinking but also becoming aware of the Truth of who we really are. The Truth that we can surrender to a God but also that that God or the Ultimate Power is within each and every one of us. There is no duality between us as humans and us as spiritual beings. We are spiritual beings having a human experience. We all started out as spirits and we chose our blueprints of what we wanted to learn and how we were going to learn these lessons in this reality before we became into our human form. Through our trials and tribulations in life, we are fulfilling the lessons that we wanted to learn before we came to this realm. When one takes responsibility and accountability for their life, it lessens the severity of the situations that their life throws at them. When you realize that you have the power to create your own reality, life becomes easier to handle.

My goal for writing this book is to help people understand that alcoholism as well as other addictions can happen to anyone. Even if someone looks like they have it all together on the outside, there can be some deep dark secrets that they are hiding. During this past year I hit rock bottom pretty hard. My ego, reputation and self-confidence were absolutely destroyed. I have fought really hard to get to where I am today. I have learned why I had an alcohol problem and I have learned some ways to build up my confidence and overcome the addiction. If my story can help one alcoholic seek help then it will be worthwhile. People have told me that my story has effected them and they do think before they drink and drive.

My brother-in-law told me that he was at his friend's house. He had had two beers and his friend asked if he wanted another one. He thought for a second about driving home and how easily an accident could happen. He said no and he went home. As he was driving home, a kid on a bike darted out in front of his car. He was able to stop in time without hitting him but he thought maybe if he had another beer he might not have been able to react as quickly.

Also, I know that my strength and courage to go through two rehab programs have given my children strength in whatever they have to face. My son said to me, "if you can get through rehab and being away from home, then I could do this." Hearing how my story and experience helps other people, really makes me feel special that God chose me as an example to help others. It has been a very emotional, psychological and spiritual battle but I know I have grown so much through the experience. I hope my story will help others realize what an addiction is, how it can destroy your life, and how through little steps you can change your life from rock bottom to self-love has been my journey. I was imprisoned by my alcoholism and I am free. I hope others can relate to my story and maybe find their freedom from their own addiction.

Chapter 1

The Accident/Jail

"**O**uch! Can you loosen these?" I asked holding back my tears. The policeman kept his eyes forward and ignored my complaints. Little beads of sweat rolled down his thick neck. It was May 31st and an extremely hot afternoon. The back of my legs stuck to the plastic back seat. The officer had an aura of arrogance. His adrenalin was high and his testosterone was even higher. I couldn't understand what satisfaction he got from humiliating and abusing me in front of my daughter and the other five students that were in the van.

The back of my legs were soaked with sweat. I tried to wiggle my body to free the skin that was stuck to the hot vinyl material. There was no way to get comfortable. I placed my head against the window with a thud wishing that I could go back in time. Just an hour or two before this whole nightmare began. My wrists were killing me. The metal of the handcuff on my right wrist was bruising my skin. My hands were tangled behind my back. I sadly looked out the window at my daughter and the other students standing helplessly and fearful at the side of the road. *What was going to happen to them? How are they going to get home?* I was responsible for them and now I was in the back seat of a police cruiser with my hands bound behind my back. The humiliation and shame were overwhelming. I wanted to wake up from this nightmare but it just kept getting worse.

That moment changed my life forever.

Just a few hours ago, we were happily driving home from a school fishing trip. The instant the motorcycle cut me off, I pumped on the brakes praying to stop in time. I was already going slowly as we were stopping at a red light. I bumped the back of his bike. I quickly got out of the van and helped the man pick up his bike. From that point on, my memory is scattered. God intervened and took away the frightening and confusing moments that followed. I remember there were police cars and a few other people who stopped to see what had happened.

The accident was so minuscule that I was shocked that it created so much attention. I asked the man if we should just exchange insurance information because there was no damage to either vehicle. I told him that I was a teacher and that we were driving home from a field trip. He instantly started complaining about his neck. I was shocked because I second before that he was fine. The police asked us to move our vehicles. I vaguely remember pulling the van to the side of the road. I know the students were upset and I tried my best to comfort them and told them that everything was going to be alright.

My daughter was furious. She kept getting in and out of the car to yell at the guy on the motorcycle. It was hard to try to control her, keep the other students calm and try to comprehend what was happening to me. The policeman had to tell her a few or so times to get back into the van. Ever since she was old enough, she always protected me. I am not sure if it was because she loved me or if it was because I appeared weak in her eyes. I tried to act cool and collective but I was scared. I had never been in a car accident before and I had no idea about the procedure. The confidence came from a power greater than me because I was in a daze. I remember the policeman was very mean and his attitude with me was awful. He asked me to sit in the cruiser. He roughly asked me a few questions and before I knew it my hands were thrown behind my back and handcuffed in front of the students and more embarrassing in front of my daughter. My arms hurt from the unexpected movement. The whole dramatic scene was so unnecessary. I was half his size. Why some men have to prove they're strong by bullying a woman is beyond me. I was so ashamed.

I remember looking at the students standing outside the van. I couldn't speak. I don't remember what was being said to me. I remember chaos and then suddenly a feeling of peace came over me and I heard a soft voice say – "it's enough, it's over". I was overcome with a sense of peace. I was overcome with tears. It was a very relaxing and calming sensation. At that moment I knew my old way of life was gone forever. I'm not sure if it was divine intervention or my Higher Power. I felt someone or something had taken over my body and my mind. I remember feeling so much gratitude and love just for a moment, then the tranquil feeling disappeared. I still wasn't mentally in my body or at the accident scene.

I looked around and it was all so surreal as if it was happening to someone else and I was watching from the outside and I was watching my own movie unfold before my eyes. I was still emotionless. It was a very bizarre yet powerful experience. People say that you only learn when you hit rock bottom. This was definitely my rock bottom. He started the police car and we drove slowly passed the students. All I could do is stare at my daughter. I remember the look of total desperation in her eyes. I could tell that she was frightened and I couldn't help her. It was awful to see that look. We drove down a few different streets. I had no idea where we were and the officer wouldn't answer any of my questions. I gave up. I shut my eyes hoping that when I opened them, I would wake up from this nightmare.

We started to slow down and he turned into the OPP Station. The ride seemed to take forever. We pulled in around back and the officer came and got me and brought me inside. I was so confused. I had no idea what was going to happen to me. Two police officers brought me downstairs. One officer undid the cuffs and I saw a black and purple bruise on my right wrist bone. It was so sore. A woman asked me a few questions and then asked for my belongings. I emptied my pockets. All I had was some change. My purse and my phone were still in the van.

I then followed another policeman to a cell. I had only seen cells on TV. It was all so unreal. I was like a zombie. *This isn't happening to me. I'm a good girl. Things like this don't happen to people like me.* I thought as I walked inside. He then shut the bars behind me with a bang. It was the weirdest feeling being locked inside. At first I imagined that I was on a sightseeing trip and that this was part of the tour. I was a little delusional overcome with fear and anxiety. I looked at the bars in terror. *I can't get out.* That was the first actual feeling that I felt since the whole incident started. *I was trapped in here. My heart started to beat faster and I was hoping that I wouldn't have a panic attack.*

The inside of the cell had faded yellow brick walls, a grey cement floor and a cement bench along the back wall. I sat down on the bench. There was a metal cylinder toilet type thing in the corner. I figured that was where I was supposed to go to the bathroom. Not a chance. It was absolutely horrible. I would not wish this on my worst enemy. It was dirty and disgusting. I know for sure that God shut off me senses at that exact moment. I was numb. I sat and just stared at the bars in front of me. No thoughts. No tears. Nothing. I'm not sure if I was in a state of shock or not. The feeling of being trapped and unable to leave was unbearable and soon I began to get extremely anxious. I started feeling claustrophobic. I never felt so helpless in my life. It's one of those memories that you wish could be taken away for ever.

I was brought out of my cell to have a breathalyser test done. One of the police officers asked me if I wanted to call a lawyer. I really didn't understand the procedure or my rights or anything. I had never been in trouble with the law before. This was all new to me. They got some lawyer on the phone. I barely remember the conversation that I had with him on the phone. He just kept telling me "blow into the machine – just blow into the machine." I started asking him question and he got angry with me. I didn't know the rules or my rights. It was awful. The lawyer hung up on me. I sat in the chair and the technician explained how the breathalyser worked. It took me so many times for the machine to register. The technician started to get mad at me.

After about twenty minutes and a million tries, they brought me back to my cell. I had no idea what time it was. The sound of the bars closing startled me. The feeling of being locked in was overwhelming. My anxiety went through the roof. I felt my heart speeding up and I started to sweat. I had a panic attack once in college and I felt another one coming on. I tried to control it. It was brutal. My head was spinning and finally I was able to divert my focus. I was worried about the kids in the van. The police didn't tell me anything. Where they were? If they were okay? It was an absolutely terrifying experience.

It started to get cold. I'm not sure if it was my anxiety or not. I asked for a blanket. The woman brought me one. It was gross. It was so rough and scratchy. I couldn't help think of all the other people who had used that blanket. Did they even wash them? I curled my legs up under me and wrapped myself in a little ball. It's funny how the brain shuts itself off when the situation is too much to handle. I'm not sure how much time went by. I could hear voices in the distance talking and laughing. A little while later the policeman said in a nasty and arrogant tone through the bars *the guy went to the hospital so now you are charged with bodily harm.* Those words went in one ear and out the other. I had absolutely no concept of what was going on.

I sat on the cement block with the blanket over my body. I was still shaking and I couldn't stop. I watched a big spider crawl along the floor. I looked at the ceiling and there were spiders everywhere. I thought I was going to be sick. It was disgusting. I walked up to the bars and asked them if I could just go home. Another male policeman came over to the bars and said that they couldn't release me because I had a car at home and they thought that I would drive it drunk. That didn't even make any sense to me.

I can't even express in words my state of mind at the time. I thank God every day for taking over my will that night because I know there is no way I could have ever survived. I had no concept of time, the lights remained on. It was getting colder in there and I was so hungry. I'm not sure if I slept or not. I didn't lay down, too many spiders and bugs. I truly believe that a Higher Power saved my life that night. I somehow made it through.

Finally, a policewoman came to the cell and asked me who she should call to pick me up. My mind was in disarray and I couldn't remember anyone's number. After a few minutes, I thought of my friend Patricia's number. Shortly after, another policewoman came to the cell. She was much harsher than the first girl. I followed her to another office and she gave me my bag with my belongings in it. She reviewed a bunch of papers with me but my mind was not there. She told me to sign at a couple of places and then she said coldly - ``you got yourself in a lot of trouble. `` I just wanted to get out of there. The energy in the whole place was so negative. I understand they were doing their job but the vibration there was very low and on the verge of evil.

The woman gave me the paper work and released me out the side door. She pointed her finger around the building and said ``your ride should becoming shortly`` and she slammed the door. It was pouring rain and freezing. I still had on my shorts, tank top and sandals from the day before. At that exact moment, I thought I was in Hell.

I waited in the cold for a few hours until my daughter came to get me. I was soaked. I had no money and no cell phone. I tried going into the police station but they wouldn`t let me go past the first door. Young women were going in and out getting police checks. I thought to myself, *they must be teachers trying to get a job.* I think they would have been floored to know that I was a teacher standing outside of a police station soaking wet. It was very embarrassing probably the lowest point in my entire life. To say that I wanted to die right there and then is an understatement.

My daughter finally showed up. She slowly got out of the car and hugged me. I knew she loved me but I was always sure that I lost her respect. She had gone to the van before she picked me up. I looked at my cell phone and dreaded the text messages that I had. No one knew about the accident yet. Thank goodness. I was hoping that it would just be brushed under the carpet and my life would go on as normal. Was I ever wrong!

Someone from the police station knew someone that I taught with years ago. He had contacted this teacher and told him that I had been arrested. Obviously this was totally against police rules but I am not surprised. This teacher decided to contact my previous students to tell them. It spread like wild fire among teenagers before it hit the papers.

I took a hot bath that night. My mind or my Higher Power wouldn't let me remember the night before. It was too tragic for me to re-live. I was in my own bed but I wasn't there. I felt as if all of this was happening to someone else and I was just an innocent bystander. It was the weirdest feeling in the world. My girlfriend, Patricia came over. She said there was a place that she wanted to take me and that I needed help. I so wish she would have helped me before the accident. She said we were going to a detox centre in St. Catharines. I had no idea what a detox center was. She said it is a place where they help people with addictions get better. That they will watch my withdrawals and help get through the first days of sobriety. *I wasn't an addict or an alcoholic. The accident could have happened to anybody. So many people had impaired charges or should have had impaired charges.* My gut told me to listen to her advice.

We drove to St. Catharines in silence. My mind was in a fog and I was exhausted. We stopped outside of an old looking house. The intake lady was amazing there. They were kind and helpful. They asked me a few questions and we made arrangements for me to be admitted the next day. I couldn't believe that I had to tell my kids where I was going and that I had a problem.

I was so ashamed and embarrassed. It's funny because as alcoholics we think we are so clever. We think we are hiding our addiction from others especially family members. The kids knew I had a problem. My daughter said, "I want my mother back." That felt like a knife ripping my heart out. I didn't know what life would be like without alcohol. It had been a part of who I was. I didn't know who I was without it. It was very scary to think of never drinking again when it had been my best friend for most of my life.

Although my kids were a little older – 20 and 18, it was still a lot for them to understand. How could this be happening to their mother? Oh, how I wanted to leave this world and never come back. I knew I would be gone for at least a week. I felt so guilty for what I had put them through but I did not know that things would get much worse. Amazingly, I still hadn't cried. It was Divine intervention, I truly believe, HE was doing for me what I couldn't do on my own. I was like a puppet on a string. I was performing the actions but my mind was trapped away not thinking.

Chapter 2
Detox & Rehab

Going to detox was the best decision I could have made in hindsight but at the time I was so confused. How could I have gone from being on a class trip to being arrested, spending a night in jail, to walking up the steps to a detox centre. It was all surreal. My boyfriend drove me on Saturday morning. For some reason, I felt that I had to walk to the front door by myself. I didn't want him to walk with me. I knew the journey ahead of me was going to be difficult but I also realized that I had to do it on my own. I am grateful for being admitted in the morning. Later that day, the accident and my name were in all of the local papers. I had made the Toronto paper and the Hamilton news. *"Local teacher charged with impaired driving on school trip"*. Now EVERYONE would know that I was a drunk. I was devastated, felt hopeless and at that moment, I did not want to live. Thank goodness that I was in detox. I didn't know how famous I had become but unfortunately my children suffered the consequences. It was only after my days in detox did I find out the embarrassment and hurt that I caused them. My son said, "They were treating us like you were dead."

I am grateful for my time spent in detox. They were helpful, kind and understanding. The nurses watched your every move to make sure the withdrawals were normal and that everyone's recovery was on the right path. I recently found out that withdrawals from alcohol can be fatal. I didn't really understand how dangerous this disease is. I met other women in there that I had only seen on the streets before and through my ignorance had labelled them. I was now spending my days and nights with these women and I soon realized how judgemental I was. We shared stories. We laughed together and we cried together. It was a small little family. No judgements just love and acceptance. I had never felt that much warmth before from people I had just met.

I realized we are all in the same boat no matter what age, colour, religion, education, financial status, and family situation we had come from. It was a very eye opening and humbling experience. I am grateful for them and the lessons they taught me. I remember one night we were sitting around the TV looking at the TV guide channel. On the side of the listings of TV shows, they had blurbs of local news, "Local high school teacher charged with impaired driving on a school trip." My jaw dropped. I literally thought I was going to die. That was the first time that I had any idea that it had made the news. That was the first time it hit me that I was in big trouble and that this was a life-changing experience. I was terrified. I remember becoming extremely introverted and suicidal thoughts crossing my mind.

That was one of the most difficult things to swallow. I had been in the paper and on the news before but that was for sports' accomplishments but to see your criminal situation scrolling on a TV screen knowing people would read and hear about your behaviour was horrible. My children came to see me in detox and now when I look back, I am not sure if that was the right thing for them to do.

I think my older two, Matt and Brooke were able to handle it but my youngest Van who was 11 at the time, probably shouldn't have come. I asked them about the papers and the news stations. They were so strong. In that moment, I wished I was dead. I had created this horrible, embarrassing situation for my children which they didn't deserve. I felt so ashamed and guilty.

I remember my young son's eyes fill with tears when he asked me if I was going to jail. I can't put into words how painful that was. I was a complete failure. How can I go from a high school teacher and basketball coach to being in detox and not knowing if your consequence will be jail? I didn't want to go outside ever. I didn't want to see anyone. Thank goodness I was in a safe environment. I was extremely depressed and detached from reality.

I recently found my journal from detox. I read the entries over and over again. It brought me back to a place that I never want to be again. I hit 'rock bottom' and I am extremely grateful for the people at detox who kept me alive. I struggled with suicidal thoughts when I was in there but their support and love made me realize that ending my life wouldn't solve anything. I am grateful for those closest to me that kept the faith even though I was distant and cold.

The first few days of sobriety were interesting. These are a few of my journal entries describing my time there. I was happy to know that after doing a lot of research, all of the symptoms I had and the emotions I experienced in detox were normal.

June 2, 2012 – *It's so cold in here. I hate being in this room. That girl beside me wasn't here when I fell asleep. This is crazy. My life is over. How am I ever going to get through this? Wow. I never thought*

I would be in a place like this. It stinks and these beds are brutal. I just want to sleep and never wake up. They are moving me upstairs. Thank goodness. Now there are three more girls here. I wonder if they are alcoholics too. She has a wicked tattoo on her arm. People like this used to scare the shit out of me. God, I just want to get away from all of this. My allergies are killing me and they won't let me have my medicine. My head is freaking pounding and I feel awful. I need a drink so bad. God please help me.

June 3, 2012 – *I've been here two days. The first two were a blur. I can't remember too much. Absolutely crazy night, super hot then super cold, sweating and freezing all night, I guess this is what they mean by withdrawal. My head is foggy. I feel so sick. I want to throw up but I can't. Why are my hands shaking so much? Stop. It's so nice to hear them say that they are proud of me. I don't know why. But it feels good; I know I couldn't stop drinking on my own. Thank goodness for Patricia, I would have never come here. It's good to hear other people's stories. I'm not the only one. The AA meetings have been great. I'm so scared of what is going to happen to me. Here, I'm safe but I'm terrified to face anyone out there. Where did I lose control? I tried on my own to stop for one or two days but then the temptation was too great. I remember waking up in the morning with a wicked hangover and telling myself – that's it – and then I would get frustrated at school and would have to pick up a bottle on the way home. That would be gone so quickly, I wonder if the girls at the wine stores ever thought I had a problem. They saw me all the time. It's been awesome the last few days not waking up feeling like shit. No headache, no nausea, no dehydration. My stomach is killing me. I feel like a whale. I have to stay strong and get through this. Why do I feel so stupid\? My brain doesn't want to work. I am having so much trouble even talking. Can all of this be withdrawal? I don't know what the hell is wrong with me. Sometimes I wish I could just leave this world.*

June 4, 2012 – *I am having a bit of a break down. Seeing my name on the news was unbearable. The people here are so kind and nice. They make you feel like you are worth something and not a failure. I look around at them and we are all struggling with an addiction. But it's in their eyes. Their soul is crying out for help. I've been around teachers for so long; I became so judgmental and arrogant. These people are the real deal. They are so sincere. I am learning so much here. What is really important in life? I know God created the accident for a reason. I am so grateful to be here. God loved me enough to give me another chance at life. HE wanted me to see the other side of life and realize that everyone is part of the Divine. I do feel peaceful like I made the right decision coming here. All of my upcoming battles with court and the board are just hurdles to see how strong my spirit and soul are. What is my true purpose in life? Why have I always felt emptiness inside of me? Did I finally realize that I have a problem? Can I now move forward on my path? It's embarrassing but sometimes we learn from our own humility. I was addicted to a substance that changed my perspective because I was too scared to face my world sober. Why did I not think I was good enough? Why have I never had any self-esteem? Why was I not confident in myself after all of my accomplishments? Was it the way I was raised? Was it the verbal abuse and lack of love from my parents? I'm sitting here on this totally uncomfortable bed looking back at my life – not in sadness but reflecting – looking for answers. I do take accountability for my actions where alcohol was involved. I have to keep reminding myself that I'm not a bad person. I wish I could think. My head is still so foggy. My stomach has gone down a bit. I'm not a whale anymore, more like a walrus. My face is getting unpuffy. It feels so good. I can't believe that guy at AA last night knew who I was from the newspaper. What is it going to be like out there? I don't know if I'm strong enough to get through this. God, help me please. I just want to die. I feel so stupid. I'm glad they said that feeling stupid is part of withdrawal. My concentration is so off and my hands and fingers are numb and tingling. This is such a weird feeling. It's funny. You* *think you are better than people because of your education or because of where you grew up. Doctor's daughter, good family, athletic scholarship to the states, Academic All-American, two Wall of Fames add criminal to this list. Very frightening. I'm sitting in detox with people I used to be scared of. People I judged as being less than me. What a bunch of shit? I am just like them. They are fighters. Their eyes have a spark of life that is missing in so many so called ``normal people`. Why did I ever think less of anyone else? How arrogant was I? What an ass I was thinking I was better? I have learned so much from their stories. They are way stronger than me. I respect them so much. I needed this wake-up call. Alcohol definitely doesn't discriminate. It can imprison anyone. I am glad this happen to me. I am becoming awake. My eyes are open and I see how stupid I was and how judgemental I was. I am humbled and I am grateful for this. Most people will continue on with their stereotypes of others. The thing with these people in detox is you can see their souls through their eyes. Beyond the tattoos and the piercing and the rough exterior, their eyes have a glow. The person inside is just like me. The women here have been so freaking supportive and accepting. It makes me cry how stupid I was to judge them before. People in the outside world will never accept what happened to me and these people love me for who I am not for what I did.*

__June 5, 2012__ – I feel a little better today. It's the first time I slept for 8 hours in a long time. I can feel the fog clear a little bit. It's only four days but I feel clearer. I don't want to have this disease anymore. I want to get better and be normal. I made a mistake because I had an addiction problem. I hope all will see that I am sick and I want help to get better. I know I am going to be faced with a lot of criticism especially by parents and the school but it was my disease not me, so hard to accept it though. The fact that I will not finish the year teaching my ESL kids is breaking my heart. I am a great teacher. Alcohol took over my life and took everything away from me. I have to make changes in my life. I need to stay positive. I am looking forward to looking back on this and knowing that it was *the turning point in my life. It was so sad seeing the kids today. Van is so upset. I must look like such a failure in their eyes. Loser. I tried so hard to be the perfect mother but doing it on your own, is brutal. Now, I've ruined their lives. How can I ever make it up to them? Poor Brooke having to face the crap at school every day. I wish they would leave her alone. I am the one that was charged and in jail. They keep taking it out on her and its so unfair. I hope that this whole experience will help my kids see that I had a problem and to learn from it. I don't want them to ever have to face what I am now facing. I wish I could run away – somewhere far – where I didn't have to face my life. My mom and dad are going to be so ashamed of me. God, where did I go wrong? Why did my life turn out so shitty? Self-pity isn't going to get me anywhere. Look at these people, they have nothing. You have kids that still love you and a house. Stop feeling sorry for yourself. It won't do any good. Look how strong these women are. Their battles are way worse than yours, and they are fighters. I gotta get through this. My head is spinning. I don't know what I am going to do. I knew I was out of control but I couldn't stop. I asked for help but nobody listened to me. I am so grateful to God for this wake-up call and that nothing more serious happened. The pain I feel right now is something I have never felt before in my life - sorrow, hurt, embarrassment, shame, guilt. Loss, sadness. My heart is so low and very sad. I miss my job. I miss my kids.*

June 6, 2012 *– I don't want to leave tomorrow. I'm so scared. I can't believe my name and the accident have been in all the newspapers and on CHCH. God, why? Why did they have to torture me like that? It's funny, when I left jail I thought this would all be swept under the carpet. Stupid thinking. Now I don't know what the hell is going to happen. I feel a little better today. My body actually looks back to normal. Wow, was I bloated? My head is still foggy. I still can't think. I hate that. So many questions and decisions to make and I feel like I'm on Mars. I guess Newport will be good rehab. Close to home and only 18 days. I can't believe I am writing this stuff like it's normal. Detox. Rehab. What the hell am I thinking* *about? I have to go see the doctor tomorrow. I know she is going to think I am exactly like my dad. He had such a bad problem. It's so embarrassing. I don't want to go home. How am I going to go anywhere in the Falls? I don't want anyone to see me. I feel like such a loser. How do you go from teacher to drunk in a day? What are my students going to think of me? Well, they really didn't have a teacher all year. I don't know how I did it. How did I get up every morning feeling like absolutely shit? - running out of the portable to puke in the garbage can outside. OMG! I am pathetic. I pray that I can get through this. I just don't see the light right now. I don't want to go home but I have to. I have to face up to this. Somehow. Why couldn't I stop? What's wrong with me? I'm in detox and I'm thinking how great a drink would be right now. God, please help me? Please! The guilt, shame, and embarrassment are overwhelming right now. The guilt I feel for putting my kids through this is unreal. I can't be seen anywhere in Niagara Falls. I need to move. Why couldn't I just stop? Why couldn't I have said `no`? It was my fault. I was very selfish. I was only thinking of myself. I could have killed someone. I have to and I will change my life. I never want to be in this situation again. What can I learn from this? How can I help others through this experience? Why did this happen?*

June 7, 2012 *– Well, I'm leaving in a bit. I can't believe what Matt told me last night. `I never expected that phone call`- that's what Matt said after he got the call from the O.P.P. that his mother had been arrested for impaired driving. This situation has to be the most embarrassing, humiliating, despicable thing I've ever been through. I feel like it happened to someone else. I don't even feel like I'm here. The embarrassment and shame tortures me. I hate that guy on the motorcycle for cutting me off. This situation ruined my life. Everything I had – is gone. I'm so sad and I'm so not used to feeling. By this time, I would have drunk and I would be numb. It's hard to control my tears right now I am so sad. I am so so sad. I'm not a bad person. I know deep down inside, I'm that little girl just looking for love. My life will never be the same.*

It can't be. I need help. I am so scared to leave. I don't want to go home. Shit. God, please help me. It's time to grow up and face life. I let so many people run my life. Always `yes`, `sure` when I didn't want too. My fault, I guess. I don't want to be here anymore. I want to leave this place and go somewhere far, far away.

Although detox was a scary and strange place for me at first, it was actually a blessing in disguise. My kids and my boyfriend at that time were able to come visit every day and I think the important people in my life knew that I was trying to make a change. They were behind me one hundred percent and they were proud of me. I went to my doctor's later in the afternoon and she did some tests to see what shape my liver was in. She knew my dad and knew of his severe alcohol and drug problem. I was so grateful that my liver hadn't sustained any damage. We talked about rehab and she made a referral to two places. I was happy later to find out that all of the symptoms that I experienced in detox: the fog in my brain, the numb sensation and tingling in my fingers and hands, the difficulty remembering and speaking and the hot and cold flashes were all part of normal withdrawal and recovery. Some of these symptoms could actually last two to three years and with some heavy drinkers these symptoms may be permanent. I am grateful mine only lasted a few weeks.

It was difficult for me in detox but I think it was much worse for my family and friends. I know they were proud of me but it must have been a very confusing time for them as well. This person they saw as strong and 'all-together' was now desperately trying to climb out of a self-inflicted hole. I am very lucky that I did not lose my children through this although my relationship with my youngest son has been strained. I am sure with time the relationship will mend.

AFTER DETOX THEN OFF TO REHAB:

Embarrassment is an understatement of how I felt after my days in detox. I didn't want to leave my house again. My license was taken away for three months so I had to rely on other people to get me to my doctor's appointments, AA meetings and court. My head was still so foggy and I felt so stupid. I remember trying to speak and the words wouldn't come out of my mouth. I would stutter and repeat myself. It was the weirdest thing. The biggest problem I was experiencing was this void. It felt like a huge part of my soul was missing. I felt empty and nothing could fill it.

My family and friends were trying to get close to me but I wouldn't let them in. It was as if I had a huge brick wall between me and the rest of the world. The only sense of freedom I felt was being in my bedroom by myself. I felt safe there. I am sure people around me wanted to give up trying. I was unresponsive and just detached from reality. I started to go to daily AA meetings. I was on the list to go to Newport Rehab. Again, like in detox, I never imagined that I would associate with people that were in AA. After my brief experience in it a few years earlier, I really had a bad image of what to expect. I was pleasantly surprised, the people in AA were accepting and kind. A few I noticed judged me when I shared my story. It had become such a part of my life, going to court, dealing with the police and lawyers, school board, losing my license, etc. that I sometimes forgot how disrespectful and horrible my charges were. Most of the AA people did not judge me though. I felt so at home among them. Those first early weeks of AA were the most beneficial to my recovery. I was still totally numb and felt outside and separated from my body. It was as if the whole situation was happening to someone else. I was just an observer. This feeling progressively got worse. I feel bad for my boyfriend. He tried so hard to get close to me and help me but I just couldn't. I felt like I was on another planet that I wasn't really here. Even thinking about leaving my house would increase my anxiety. I know this was very difficult for those close to me. I had become a recluse and extremely introverted. I couldn't explain this void that I was feeling.

I remember the first time I went to court in Cayuga. I worked for a law firm a long time ago so I had been to court on a few occasions but not as a criminal. The atmosphere and the lawyers' aura were so overwhelming. The negativity of the room gave me chest pains. I brought my quartz crystal and I held on to it so tightly. I felt like a degenerate. Again, God or a Higher Power took over that day. I couldn't face it emotionally, psychologically or physically. There were a few occasions when I wanted to end it all. I couldn't handle the pressure. My family and friends were trying to understand but I continually shut down and hid from reality.

TREATMENT

I knew I had a drinking problem but I never thought I was an alcoholic. *My parents were alcoholics and I didn't want to admit that I was like them. They were abusive alcoholics; I wasn't abusive to my kids. So I must not be an alcoholic – wishful thinking!* After the experience of the accident and jail, I realized that I needed help. I started my journey at a detox centre. Prior to that Friday night, I did not even know what a detox centre was. I thought it was some health spa type deal to lose weight but soon enough I found out. I met wonderful people there - non-judgemental and kind. We were all in the same boat – all addicts – although we were so different: backgrounds, family life, education, employment, social status and religion. It was a real eye-opening experience for me. I didn't think that I was better than addicts before, I just could never think of myself as one of them.

My ego wouldn't allow me to think that I could possibly be in that category. Addicts and alcoholics were bad people who want to live on the streets or in shelters. It never occurred to me what the truth was. Once I let my ego thinking go, I was able to learn so much from the other women there and from the counsellors. So many people have dramatic stories of their childhoods and lives. I am so impressed with their determination and perseverance to get through their situations. Getting to know some of these people, gave me the strength and hope that I would make it through this adventure.

Between detox and rehab, I slowly got worse and worse. I separated myself from those closest to me. The void I felt was unreal. I was detached from reality. Every day I woke up hoping that the nightmare was over. The fog in my brain was still heavy and I had absolutely no feelings. I can't believe that those around me kept on supporting me. I am very grateful for them. If I didn't have the support, I would have ended my life. I am positive about that.

I went to Newport Centre, a rehabilitation establishment in Port Colborne in July – eighteen days, no visitors, no leaving the premises just locked in. It was on the shores of Lake Erie. The view was amazing. I was there in the summer so most of our time was spent outside. We played volleyball and basketball. It was a wonderful place. There were ten other women and eleven men. I learned so much about myself there and about my alcoholism. I learned that I had many insecurities and fears about life. I was living in the past which had control over my present thoughts and actions. Like many alcoholics, I had very low self-esteem and self-confidence. Drinking was the crutch that I needed to have that out-going personality and self-assurance. It was only when I was drunk did I exhibit these traits.

It was scary being there at first. Although my kids were older, it was the first time that I had left them by themselves for more than four days. I was worried about them and about my dog. I kept trying to convince myself that I was on vacation not in a rehab facility. My kids had to grow up pretty quickly. I still feel very guilty for putting them through this. I remember this one day the counsellor asked us to talk about things that we had accomplished in our lives. I shyly said about my books that I had written and my successes in basketball and school. I am not sure if I mumbled. I remember feeling my face heat up because I was so embarrassed to speak in front of 22 people. This young guy looked at me and said out loud – "What the hell is wrong with you? Were you abused or something as a kid?" I was shocked. "If I did half of what you accomplished, I would be telling everybody." It was at that point that I realized how low my alcohol dependency had taken me.

I couldn't see in myself what a stranger saw within five minutes. I am grateful for that day and what he said. Every time I start criticizing myself, I hear his voice saying – "What the hell is wrong with you?"

Another coping skill they taught me to help with self-esteem is to find a picture of yourself as a child and place the picture where you would see it – in the mirror in the washroom, bedroom mirror or screen saver on the computer. I have a picture as my background on my phone. It is a picture of me in kindergarten. I think I was five or six years old. It is the typical one you get at school. They make you pose on a chair and they snap a picture. The process is every time I start saying something negative about myself, I look at the picture and ask: *Would you say that to the little girl in the picture?* It breaks my heart because I see the innocence in the little girl's eyes. I see a little girl with so much potential and so much trust. It really helps put things into perspective for me. It has really helped me a lot with my negative self-talk and my low self-esteem.

After Newport Rehab, I knew I had changed. I felt my self-esteem had increased a little bit and I was a little more assertive. Even though I felt different, I was returning to a life and a home that hadn't changed. Shortly after I returned home, the void feeling returned. I was protected in Newport. It was like living in a bubble and then when I came home, reality of my situation hit me again. It wasn't as intense as it had been before but it was still there. I became more introverted and I only felt at peace when I was alone. I am sure my kids didn't understand what was happening to me. Greg, my boyfriend at the time, and I began to fight. He tried everything to get me to open up and I just couldn't. He tried to get me out of the house. We fought and fought. I would get angry and make excuses to spend more time in my bedroom by myself. To be honest, I thought I would never get better. I thought my mind and my feelings would never come back. I had absolutely no feelings – good or bad. I was completely numb. I know I shut everyone out. I am glad that they didn't give up on me at that time. I realized how important it was to have supportive loving people around even at that time I didn't appreciate them.

After Newport Rehab, I continued to attend AA meetings. At this time, I also started having weekly sessions with a psychologist. We talked about the things that I was lacking in my life – self-esteem, self-worth, setting boundaries, and being assertive. I continued to feel a void in my life it was the weirdest feeling. I wasn't sad or happy. I wasn't positive or negative. I was just there. I couldn't feel anything. I couldn't recall the details of the accident without breaking down in tears. I became even more introverted and I pushed friends and family away. I remember this one time asking at an AA meeting, what was wrong with me. I was so confused and depressed. The void was huge and I couldn't see anything positive in my future. A few of the old-timers assured me that the void numb feeling was just part of recovery. *Your brain has to adjust to no alcohol.* Some of the other alcoholics had this numb feeling for years after they stopped drinking. I started questioning myself – *What damage have I done to my brain? Why did I drink so much for all those years? Why didn't seeing my parents drunk deter me from drinking? How is this going to affect the kids? Of course, then the questioning lead to – Why am I such a loser? What is wrong with me? Wouldn't their lives be better without me? It was a vicious cycle.*

This was a very difficult time for me. I wasn't working. I was on sick leave and the school board threatened me on a few occasions that they were going to stop paying me. My mother was progressively getting worse. My financial troubles were increasing. My daughter had gotten into trouble at school with the vice principal. I think my daughter was hiding her embarrassment and disappointment in me by acting rebellious. As a result of her behaviour at school, she was not allowed to attend her own graduation. I felt so guilty for that. I know she was sticking up for me. The VP's were questioning the students about the accident and were also threatening some of the students that their future university careers would be in jeopardy if they did not tell the truth. That manipulation was so unfair to these students.

The funny thing is, the students were telling the truth but the VP's wanted to hear the story that they concocted in their heads. It was like the whole world was against me and my kids. It was an absolute horrible time. I still had not left the house. My daughter did the groceries and other errands for me. It wasn't fair to my kids but I couldn't face the outside world. I was so scared. I wanted to be alone. I wanted to isolate from everything and everyone. They had already crucified me in the papers and on the news. I couldn't take any more humiliation.

I went to court in August. I thought I was better with my anxiety but I wasn't. We pulled into the courthouse parking lot and I lost it. I wouldn't get out of the car. I was crying hysterically. Greg was very supportive and a blessing at that time. He spoke to my lawyer. Eventually, I calmed down. The drive home from Cayuga was very dramatic. Greg had to pull over to the side of the road. Everything that had been building up, came out. I absolute lost it. If Greg wasn't there, I'm sure I would have done something stupid. Without him throughout this whole ordeal, I don't think I would have survived. Greg and I remain close friends to this day and without friends or family, recovery can be lonely and scary. No one understood and no matter how I tried to explain my detached feelings, I was fortunate that no one gave up on me.

By the time I was contacted by Homewood, I had started to slowly forgive myself for the accident and for the pain and hurt I had caused my kids. I was going to therapy to try to get the courage to accept the accident and the criminal charges against me. I wasn't living at all. I was just existing. I felt totally numb. I was really scared that I was never going to get better.

I went to Homewood Rehabilitation Centre in Guelph on October 25, 2012. This was a thirty-five day rehab based on the 12-step program. It was an incredible experience. The self-growth and awareness I learned there was phenomenal. The hardest thing for an alcoholic to accept – is the truth. I am very grateful for the opportunity to have thirty-five days to work on me. I was embarrassed to be in rehab but I was also excited that I could release and let go of all the circumstances and feelings that I had repressed since childhood. The power of discussing your deep secrets and fears and letting them go, opens up a whole new area of your existence. *Secrets make you Sick.* I was holding onto some very damaging self-concepts learned in childhood. Once I was able to talk about my repressed feelings, the power they had over me vanished.

Although it was a difficult process, I know I needed to address these issues in order to maintain a sober life. Being an alcoholic and always covering up my feelings, I wasn't aware of the hidden emotions I had built up. Homewood focused on feelings and expressing those feelings. I learned so much about myself through this program. It did change my life because I was able to release the past and recognize that it didn't have control over me anymore. It was very easy to feel 'normal' at Homewood. It was like being in a little pink bubble. It was not reality. After five weeks, I was very nervous returning home. Again, I may have changed but I was returning to my past life.

Homewood taught me a very deep rooted behaviour that I had been carrying around my entire life. I subconsciously was seeking the male attention that I didn't receive from my father. My two failed marriages and my numerous failed relationships all stemmed from my need for male attention that I lacked growing up. The counsellors were hard on me and at first I got very angry because deep down I knew that what they were trying to make me see, was true. I needed to become aware of what vibes I send out when I interact with men. I took this as an insult at first but after I thought about it, I considered that maybe I was doing that subconsciously to get their attention. Since then, I have become aware of my actions when I do interact with men. I have noticed a difference in myself. There is definitely a boundary I now put up which before I didn't because I didn't have that awareness or the coping skills. Also, being an alcoholic, I was never fully conscious or aware of my daily actions.

"No matter how much damage your addiction has done – to your health, your emotions, your family, your career, your finances – you can pick up the pieces of your life and build a strong, healthy sobriety. But sobriety

doesn't happen overnight. It takes effort and time – and it takes a plan, so that that effort and time is spent profitably." (Restore Your Life – A Living Plan for Sober People)

That quote is so true. Making changes in your life will not happen over- night. I was an alcoholic for many years. I developed certain brain patterns and life coping skills all based around alcohol. Now, through both rehab programs, I am able to confront my life sober and I have learned to release the past and live for today. I know I have changed but I also face a society that stereotypes people who are addicts and more importantly people who have been to rehab. People that I will have to confront whether it will be at court or the school board,all have a preconceived notion of what an alcoholic is and what type of people attend rehab. That is the hardest thing to comprehend now. I am an alcoholic. I have been to detox and two rehab programs. I have criminal charges against me. We live in a world that doesn't accept this very easily. I know I will be judged for my behaviours not for the person I truly am. That makes me sad but I know I have the strength and the life skills now to overcome the potential judgements that awaits me.

Chapter 3

. . . .

Where Did This All Begin

I want to point my finger at others and blame them for my situation. I want to say it's all their fault for raising me wrong or doing this and that to me. But that is not the truth. I caused my own problems and I created this situation in order to learn. After 47 years I was able to finally see the truth. Believe me I blamed my parents, my family, my ex-husbands, my boyfriends, my friends, and my kids. I was kind of hard on my dog once in a while too.

Like a lot of alcoholics, I was raised in a Catholic family. I was the youngest of seven children. I had six older sisters and one brother – he was the oldest. It was your typical dysfunctional alcoholic family. I say I was raised Catholic but my parents never went to church. They made us go but I don't remember them ever taking us. We went sometimes for midnight mass on Christmas Eve. We had no role models to follow so going to church really was meaningless. My sisters and I would skip Sunday mass and go to Tim Hortons or just for a walk. We had to get the bulletin though so that our parents thought we went. Each week it was someone else's turn to run into the back of the church, grab a bulletin and run back out. I went to Catholic school and was taught to fear God.

I was taught that bad behaviour would lead me to Hell. Sex was bad and any negative behaviour would be punished. I took that very seriously. I was *very good* girl. I didn't drink or do any drugs. I didn't even know what sex was. I was very naïve and socially ignorant. I was scared of my mother and father. I was scared to get in trouble at home or at school. Fear, fear, fear – everywhere in my life. We had a bathroom upstairs that had no windows. During thunder storms, I would take my blanket and pillow and lay on the floor in the bathroom. I felt so safe there. That was the safest place for me in that house.

Looking back, I would have had some fun during my childhood instead of always fearing the wrath of God. My father was a surgeon and my mother stayed home to raise us. Happy memories of family times are far and few between. I remember the drinking and I remember the fighting. It was terrifying. I hated listening to them yell at each other. My dad sometimes hit my mom. It was a horrible place to grow up. I remember I used to run. When my parents started to fight, my sister who I shared a room with, would go downstairs and stand in between them. I would get up and run to my friend's house.

According to my mother, I never knew my dad. He had a brain aneurysm in 1966. I was only a year old. My mother always told me that `your father died in 1966` and she didn`t marry this man who now lived in our house. It was a horrible thing to say to a child. My father`s personality supposedly changed. I don`t remember him either way. I just remember him being drunk most of the time.

My next older sister and I used to plead with the older siblings to stay home at night. We knew that as soon as the older kids were gone, the fighting would begin. I remember this one night. They were fighting and I'm not sure why my mother got my sister and I involved. But she put us in the bathroom with her and jammed the door with two knives that she had with her. I remember my father yelling outside the door and I remember crying. I still have no idea what happened that night.

Eventually my mother kicked my father out when I was fourteen years old. Although the yelling and fighting at night stopped, it was also when my mother started drinking more heavily. My sister and I would walk home from school after basketball practice. We never knew what we would face. If the house was pitch black and opera music blaring than we knew that my mother was drunk. We would sit outside until she opened the door. We would have five minutes to run upstairs and into our bedroom. No dinner. No discussion. Nothing. We had to keep up the image of being a doctor's family but inside those walls, life was horrible.

I spent most of my time playing basketball or working out. I needed something to keep me away from the house. In high school, I played on a basketball team that practiced every day except Christmas. I remember asking my coach if it was possible to practice that day because I didn't want to be home. Our Christmas' after my dad left were filled with Gordon Lightfoot or Cat Stevens music. The house was decorated but lacked any sense of peace or joy. No one ever really knew what was going on inside our house. On the outside, all of us turned out to be very successful.

We hid our pain and suffering well – or so I thought. People often tell me now that they knew what was going on in the house. I'm sure our friends and neighbours knew the truth. I ended up getting a scholarship to Wheeling Jesuit College to play basketball and to go to school in West Virginia. It was very exciting and I was very happy to be away from home. I did really well in school and ended up having a very successful basketball and educational career.

But then it was time to come back home. I tried every way possible to extend my VISA to stay in West Virginia but I had to come back to Canada. Being a child of two alcoholics, there was never any guidance or direction from my parents. I had so much going for me. A university education, a 3.6 grade point average, graduated Cum Laude, Academic All-American two years in a row, and numerous other awards and accomplishments but it was never enough. I never felt good enough. I never felt love or acceptance from my parents.

This one time I met my dad at a bar in Welland. I was on a date with a new boyfriend. My dad was drunk of course. I remember being really embarrassed. At one point, my father looked at me and said, " I wish you weren't my daughter". I was mortified. I immediately left. I look back at all of my relationships with men. I never felt good enough for them. I think it was because I had spent my entire life trying to get my father's attention. That night he gave me attention but not the paternal kind that I had lacked growing up. I was so angry. At that time, I did not understand alcoholism or addiction. I now know that my father was an alcoholic and unaccountable for his actions.

A few months later, I started dating my first husband. I was drinking a lot at this time and I started having blackout. On a drunken night in Hamilton, I got pregnant. My dreams of going to law school and becoming a criminal lawyer vanished instead we got married. We had two children together. I was unhappy and I resented the fact that this was my life. I worked at a law firm as a legal assistant. I was drinking quite heavily at this time. I didn't want to be married. I thought I was missing out on my late 20's partying and I resented having a husband and kids. We got a divorce four years later. I don't blame him at all. We really didn't have a marriage. I was miserable, resentful and consequently drunk most of the time. I sold the house and the kids and I moved into my sister's basement. I was so grateful. We had nowhere else to go.

My other sister lived in Rochester, New York. One weekend, I went down to visit her. I met a doctor there. We dated and he offered to rent a townhouse there. I was flattered. Someone thought I was pretty and loved me. My low self-esteem and neediness lead me towards this relationship. He was fifteen years older than me. So I moved to Rochester with my three and a half year old son and fifteen –month old daughter. He gave me his credit card and I bought a new bed set, bunk beds and furniture for this new place. He didn't move in with me. He came to visit me a couple of times a week and that was it. I somehow was able to only work at the law firm three days a week. I would drive from Rochester (a two hour drive) to Welland, drop the kids off at my mother's, work all day and then drive the two hours back.

My drinking increased quite a bit. I didn't understand what I was doing. I was in another country being pretty much bought and paid for with my two little kids. After two and a half months, I decided that this wasn't for me. I packed up my things and took the final drive to Welland. Fortunately, my mother let me and the kids move in with her. It was great. I would put the kids to bed and then I went out drinking with my friends. One night when my sister and I were out, I met my second husband at a bar (big surprise). He was playing guitar with his friend. He sent over another bottle of red wine to keep us at the bar. I couldn't leave a free bottle of wine. Right? The relationship progressed quicker than expected. We decided to get married in the Bahamas. I remember going to work on the Friday. My co-worker asked me what I was doing on the weekend. I told her nonchalantly that I was going to Bahamas to get married. Her jaw dropped. It was crazy and she knew that I wasn't really into him. Anyway, being an alcoholic and a people pleaser, I went along with it and we got married. I am not sure why I just kept agreeing when deep down I knew it wasn't the right thing to do.

Again, I wasn't happy. I remember sitting at the kitchen table every morning trying to figure out how I could get out of the marriage. That is around the time that I started hanging around with my single friends. My husband and I soon split up and I was single again. My marriages never went beyond the four and a half year mark. I wasn't happy and I didn't like myself. I had no self-esteem at all. That's what I liked about drinking. When I drank this confident, out-going and fun person came out. I liked that person. I stupidly thought I would get self-fulfillment from being married and having children. But now I was divorced twice, and responsible for three children.

I love both of my ex-husbands. They put up with a lot of drunken nights and some very angry and hurtful comments from me. Divorced twice, in Rochester once, dating guy to guy to guy, and still I wasn't happy. I was lacking something in my life and the drinking continued. I was still in somewhat in control of my life at this time.

My father passed away of lung cancer on September 1, 2000 (my birthday – September 1). I was able to forgive him on his death bed. I told him that I always loved him and I asked why he never loved me back. He didn't respond. Right after he passed, an amazing experience happened to me. That was the first time I knew there was something greater in the universe than myself. I knew there was a Higher Power protecting me through that time period. I remember standing my father's bed side. I watched him take his last few breaths and then he died.

My father and God knew that I physically could not handle death. While I was standing by his bed, a calmness spread throughout my body. It started at my feet and travelled to the top of my head. I didn't cry and I wasn't sad. I looked at my other sisters and comforting words came out of my mouth that weren't mine. I was saying things to people that I would never have known about.

The weirdest thing was my father was supposed to be cremated and his ashes thrown in the water off of the Nova Scotia coast. But I kept telling my sisters no. That dad wants to be buried under a tree in a grave yard in Fonthill. My two older sisters looked into the local cemetery and sure enough they found a plot under a tree in Fonthill.

This incredible experience lasted about five hours. My body was the same but inside I was someone else. It was the weirdest yet most calming thing I have ever been through. I am grateful that my dad and God did take that away from me. It was horrible watching him die. There weren't many people at my dad's funeral. The few that were there told me that my dad did his best surgery while drunk. Not the kind of memory your children really want to hear. I remember leaving the cemetery that day. I turned my head and stared at my dad's plot until it was out of view. I felt bad for leaving him. The whole experience was very surreal.

At this time, I was a single mother, I had three kids, I was struggling financially and trying to keep my head above water. I had a close friend who had recently gotten separated. We worked together and I really admired how confident she was. I was jealous that she had grown up in a normal family and didn't have all of the insecurities that I had. I remember asking her about her upbringing. She told me that her parents were loving and kind and very supportive. No wonder she was so confident and out-going. By this time, I had very low self-esteem and lacked confidence. I felt like a failure. It is incredible how many people judge others for being divorced. Two divorces and it is like you committed a crime. I hated being judged for decisions that I knew deep down were right.

My friend introduced me to a few other divorced women and the four of us became inseparable. We talked to each other about everything. Our kids were around the same age. We did things all together, celebrated different holidays and we created our own little family. We had a lot of fun. The drinking and partying was in full gear and that's when the blackouts started getting worse. I remember waking up Saturday morning not remembering a thing from the night before. Sometimes I would wake up on the bathroom floor and sometimes I would be in my bed with absolutely no memory of either.

The first thing I would do is make sure that the kids were okay. I didn't remember what time I got home and even sometimes how I got home but it was always a relief when I found them safe. The next thing I would do is check the drunken text messages I sent and try to remember parts of the evening. Sometimes I could and other times there was nothing in my memory from the night before. I was an early riser drunk or not. I was always so jealous of those people that could sleep in after a night out and sleep through most of their hangovers.

My hangovers were brutal. I think back to those days and wonder how I ever survived. I would always swear to myself "no more, I am done drinking." But by around 4:00 in the afternoon when the hangover was gone, I felt marvellous and I would make plans to go out again and obviously drink. We usually spent a good hour or two reviewing the night before. Between us, we were able to reconstruct the night.

It was a crazy lifestyle for about two years. I had a blackout situation where I embarrassingly do not remember what happened.

Needless to say, I knew I was in bad shape. I didn`t have to read any books on figuring out if I had a problem or not. I went to an AA meeting the next night. I met a guy named George there. He brought me to meetings and helped me look at the steps. We went to a closed meeting and I said - ``Hi, I`m Frankie. `` And that's it. The words – *I'm an alcoholic* - would not come out of my mouth. George stood up for me but I could tell that they did not want me to stay.

I continued to go to meetings with George until I noticed that his feelings for me had changed. He was still concerned about my sobriety but he had developed some romantic feelings. Things between got a little awkward and I quit going to AA at all and I cut off all ties with George.

By this time, I had three months under my belt and I figured I could control my drinking. I thought I would try soda water mixed with wine – a spritzer. That would keep my drinking under control. Soon enough I was mixing one part soda water to eight parts wine. I then had a great idea. I started drinking coolers but the problem was I had to drink a lot of coolers for any effect. My waist slowly started getting bigger and bigger. Then of course it was back to my old-time favourite – vodka and water with a slice of lemon. I was drinking water; it had to be good for me, right? Obviously not.

The craziness started up again and soon enough my blackouts were increasing as well. I couldn`t do anything or go anywhere without being totally drunk. I would place a glass of wine on my table beside the TV when I worked out. When the instructor said ``get some water``, I would drink some wine. I couldn`t go see my son`s band unless I was drunk. The one thing I never did was drink during school hours. I never drank while teaching or during the school day. I was actually proud of this fact back then, now I see how insane my thinking was. I couldn`t keep a steady boyfriend. Alcohol made me fun and flirty. Even if I had a boyfriend, I would piss him off when we were at the bar that by the end of the night, I didn't have a boyfriend anymore.

I didn't care about anything or anybody: my kids and my girlfriends. Life was a little out of control but still manageable. In March 2006, my girlfriend who had helped me so much get out of the rut I was in had a brain aneurysm. It devastated me. The only way that I could go to see her in the hospital is if I was drunk. Then I would leave the hospital crying and upset. A couple hours later when I sobered up a bit, I couldn't remember my visit at all. That was the beginning of the end. My friend did not get any better. I avoided seeing her because I selfishly couldn't. That is one my biggest regrets that I gave into the insecurity instead of caring about how I might be helping her.

For the last five years prior to the accident, I was dating a friend from high school. After a few months he saw a difference in me when I drank. He made it very clear that if I drank, our relationship would be over. So, what did I do? I hid it from him. I hid bottles in cupboards and in coffee cups. I carried toothpaste and mint gum in my purse. I continued to drink even though I knew the consequences if he found out. I got really good at hiding the bottles, or so I thought.

Every Tuesday night I had to put out the recycling and garbage. I put my empty bottles in other people's recycling boxes. No one ever knew. I thought I was being tricky but my kids later told me that they knew I was drinking a lot and I think he did as well. Through the next four and a half years, I drank whenever I could.

By the end, I didn't care if he knew or not. I hadn't seen my friend for a few years. My kids were getting older and more defiant. My finances were in rough shape and my mother had to have heart surgery. We would get calls from the hospital that my mom had fainted again. Several times at the hospital, my mother would say she just wanted to see everyone before she died. She always thought she was dying. School was fulfilling but I always felt that I should be doing more with my life. I was good at teaching the English as a Second Language (ESL) students and I enjoyed it immensely. I had no friends. I rarely spoke to my family. My life revolved around when my boyfriend was going to be home next. My life had become unmanageable. I was heavily drinking by this time. I didn't even bother hiding it from my boyfriend. I was able to get this case of Italian wine for $60.00 bucks and I would go through the bottles like they were water. My tolerance had increased so high that even after five bottles of wine some nights I still wanted more. I didn't want to feel anything. I wanted to be free of my thoughts.

In January 2012, after almost five years, my boyfriend woke up one morning and said that he wasn`t the right guy for me and left. That was it – the spiral of destruction began. I never even thought us breaking up was a possibility. We had talked about getting a house together and going on trips. I was devastated.

The first few months after he left, I spent in my room drinking numerous bottles of wine a night. I slept with the lights on and I just cried. I either ended up passing out in bed or spending sometime hugging the toilet. In March, I finally started sleeping with the lights off. My friend had told me about her on-line dating experience so I decided to give it another try. I had been on dating sites before - lots and lots of drunken encounters that I can't bear to mention. I still had my profile on the site from a few years earlier so it was rather easy to get back in the swing of things. *Nothing like a couple bottles of wine searching for Mr. Right while sitting on your couch.* Could life get any better! I was trying to find my happiness outside of myself once again.

I was so self-absorbed that I actually believed what these guys on the site were saying – "I finally found my true love", "Where have you been all my life." It didn't even faze me that that was their pick-up line to every girl on the site. I went on a few dates. I can't remember most of them. I would polish off a bottle or two at my house. Then meet my date out at a bar and we would drink a few more glasses of wine. I would make it home somehow most of the time not remembering any of my conversation with them. That's when the throwing up started to increase. I spent more time on my bathroom floor then in my bed. I still would wake up in the morning, walk the dogs and go to school. I felt horrible but I never called in sick. There were a few occasions at school where I had to run out of the portable to throw up in the garbage can outside.

I was in rough shape. By this time, it would be easy for me to polish off five to six bottles of wine a night and sometimes still want more. I was out of control and spiralling pretty quickly. I remember asking some people for help or hoping that they would stop me but no one did. I don't blame anyone for that. I was selfish at that time. I'm sure I wasn't the best mother, sister or friend either – I had shut everyone out of my life. I've never asked my kids or my friends, what I was like at that time. I'm not sure I really want to know.

This was where I was in my life before the accident. I just agreed with people even if it wasn't what I wanted to do. I had no self-worth or self-esteem but when I drank I was outgoing and confident. I don't think I have ever been to a wedding or a special party or dinner sober. A concert? Forget it! I don't remember the songs they played or even being at most of the concerts I've been too. I had the cool experience of dancing with Prince onstage – I don't remember. And my conversation with Bono in a bar in Toronto is gone from my memory.

I think back at all the important milestones in my life and my children's lives that I wasn't mentally there to experience them or remember them. I was awarded two 'Wall of Fames' – one for my high school and one for my university. I don't remember either ceremony. Looking back at my life and all of my mistakes, I felt that I needed to find out why.

Chapter 4

What I have learned about My Disease

When a person first hears the word alcoholic immediately they think of the stereotypical drunk - *a dirty person wearing ripped and torn clothing living on the streets huddled in doorways of dark alleys late at night clutching onto a paper bag.* But is this stereotype valid? I am sure we have all driven by a person before and said, "That's an alcoholic." Alcoholics are easy to pick out of a crowd of people, aren't they? Have you ever asked yourself what does a true alcoholic look like? Once upon a time the alcoholic could be spotted a mile away. They had a stigma that followed them, one of homelessness and vagrancy. These people were less than human to most and were often outcast from society. These people were thought to have made bad choices that resulted in their destitution and alcoholism. This is not the case anymore.

A stereotypical description of an alcoholic as stated above certainly is the easiest way to compare your-self to and affirm to yourself

– "No, I'm not one of those people. I don't look like that. I'm not an alcoholic," and the illusion of 'being normal' is affirmed.

The truth is as written in AA Big Book (page 17) describing the types of alcoholics. *"We are average Americans. All sections of this country and many of its occupations are represented, as well as many political, economic, social and religious backgrounds. We are people who normally would not mix."*

Admitting that one is an alcoholic is extremely difficult. *Why me? Why am I not normal?* Grasping this concept of being abnormal is very confusing for an alcoholic. Not "being normal" leads to feelings of isolation, low self-esteem, low self-worth and low self-confidence.

"Most of us have been unwilling to admit we were real alcoholics. No person likes to think he is bodily and mentally different from his fellows." A.A. page 39

In our society, *not being normal* can be viewed as a sign of weakness and inadequacy. An alcoholic does not admit they are an alcoholic until they are confronted with the realization that they have a problem. It may take losing a job, a wife / husband, children, reputation, pride and of course the ultimate - death. People do not want to admit they have a problem but once alcohol is in their system and the changes in their personality occur, it becomes quite apparent.

"But what about the real alcoholic? He may start off as a moderate drinker; he may or may not become a continuous drinker; but at some stage of his drinking career he begins to lose all control of his liquor consumption, once he starts to drink."

What is the difference between `normal drinking` and `problem drinking`? I asked myself this over and over again. Yes, that is the first sign. If you start wondering and asking yourself if you have a drinking problem then you probably do. Normal drinkers do not question the possibility.

In the book *Alternatives to Abstinence* , Heather Ogilvie states that *problem drinking is alcohol consumption that leads to recurring incidents of violence, legal trouble, hospital admittance, drunken driving arrests and accidents, marital and family problems and employment problems.* These are usually situations where the alcoholic hits `rock bottom`. Basically, a person has a problem with alcohol when they cannot stop drinking. Blackouts are a huge sign that something isn`t right. Dependency on alcohol to cope with life is a sign that there may be a problem.

As stated in Alcoholics Anonymous, *"Despite all we can say, many who are real alcoholics are not going to believe they are in that class. By every form of self-deception and experimentation, they will try to prove themselves exceptions to the rule, therefore non-alcoholic. If anyone who is showing inability to control his drinking can do the right-about-face and drink like a gentleman, our hats are off to him. Heaven knows, we have tried hard enough and long enough to drink like other people."* (Page 31 – AA)

Denial, denial, denial will keep the alcoholic sick. Once the alcoholic comes to grips and admits he/she has a problem and is an alcoholic then their life begins to improve. The hardest part of having an addiction to any substance is admitting it.

"One aspect of our addiction was our inability to deal with life on life's terms. We tried drugs (or alcohol or other addictive behaviours) to cope with a seemingly hostile world. We dreamed of finding a magic formula that would solve our ultimate problem – ourselves." N.A. page 4

Alcoholism is a disease. Society does not see it that way. Society sees alcoholism and addiction as a moral weakness. Alcoholics are seen as somewhat inferior to the general public. Society's negative view of what an alcoholic is further deters the alcoholic to admit their problem.

There are signs that an alcoholic recognizes in him or herself that makes them question if they are an alcoholic. Below is a general list of symptoms of an alcoholic. I read these symptoms and thought if I exhibited any of the behaviours. I listed my own experiences with some of the symptoms. You do not have to have all of the symptoms to be an alcoholic. Although it was difficult, I was able to relate to many of the symptoms and I finally had to admit to myself that I had a problem.

According to the *Diagnostic and statistical Manual of Mental Disorders (DSM)* common **symptoms of addiction** include:

a) *Tolerance – the need to behave in the addictive behaviour more and more to get the desired effect;*

By May 2012, I was able to drink four to five bottles of wine between 3:30 and 9:00 o'clock every day. Some nights this was not enough. I didn't feel anything from that much alcohol. So, I would drive to the Wine Rack to get another bottle or two. That was a real shock to me. I couldn't believe how much I was able to drink and not feel drunk at all.

b) *Avoiding withdrawal – with some drugs and alcohol, the dependent person must keep using in order to not experience withdrawal symptoms. Withdrawing is uncomfortable and can be life-threatening. Symptoms such as nausea, restlessness, insomnia, depression, sweating, shaking, anxiety and seizures can be part of a person's withdrawal.*

I remember the few days that I didn't drink, I was so irritable. No matter what the kids did, I snapped at them even if it was my own fault. Insomnia and sweating were nightly rituals on those few evenings that I didn't drink. I would get horrible headaches and felt nauseous and shaky during the day. I had trouble sleeping. All I kept thinking of was having a drink. It was a horrible obsession. As soon as I had a drink, the headache, nausea and the anxiety disappeared.

c) *Loss of control – the substance use has a hold on you – like a true love. It's all you think about and dream about. You tell yourself you're not going to use that much or at all, but you give in losing the battle once again. The addict asks themselves – 'do I have a problem?' A non-addict does not ask themselves these types of questions. The minute a person starts questioning their behaviour the line between addict and non-addict has been crossed.*

It's funny what I thought was normal behaviour was absolutely insane. I don't think normal drinkers switch wine stores nightly so that the wine store clerk wouldn't think that they drank so much. The worst thing was when the clerk worked at two different stores. I would be shocked and come up with an excuse for why I was buying two more bottles even though I just bought two the night before.

I started to date during the last couple of months of my insanity. I was out of control. I would drink before I went on any dates. My standards were definitely lowered and impaired. I allowed these men to treat me poorly. I didn't know any better. I hadn't had a sober date in years. I look back at some of the dates and the parts that I remember were pretty bad. Some of my behaviour during this time frame is too embarrassing to write in this book. Things I wouldn't want my kids to know about their mother. So many times I asked myself what was wrong with me. I was at a point in my life where it was totally unmanageable and totally out of control. Near the end of my drinking career, there wasn't a day that went by that I did not drink. I would be proud of myself if I only had one or two bottles of wine instead of four or five bottles. I am very happy that my brain can't remember vivid details of that time frame.

d) *Social, occupational or recreational activities becoming more focused around the addiction and important social and occupational roles being jeopardized;*

I am grateful that I never relied on drinking in the morning or during work hours. I was hung over most of the time but I never drank. I taught high school students. I took my job very seriously and I really enjoyed teaching. That was the only part of my life that I look forward too. Near the end, that as well faded. I began to dislike the students and the school.

e) *Neglect – nothing matters except for when and where you are going to use drugs or alcohol. Planning takes more time, so other responsibilities get dropped and using becomes priority.*

My day was occupied with when and where my next drink was going to be. I would think about if I wanted red wine or white wine all day. After I finished work at 2:30, I took the same road home every day. Depending on which day it was, I would stop by the 'daily' wine store and got my stash for the night. I forced myself to work out every day. I made a deal with myself. *If you work out, you can drink.*

It made the drinking so much more enjoyable. Any chore I had to do around the house or doing school work was always easier with a glass or two of wine. I don't know if they ever believed me or not. It was a crazy façade to keep up. I was obsessed with drinking that my workout routine soon went by the wayside. I picked up a bottle on the way home from work and it was usually done by the time I finished making dinner. By that time, I couldn't work out, I would have to go get more wine to conquer the rest of the night.

f)   *Inability to stop – the addicted person knows that the use is out of control and it's bad for them, but continues to use regardless of the consequences: blackouts, illnesses, depression, paranoia, seizures, skin lesions, anxiety.*

Every time that I drank in April and May, I would have blackouts. I couldn't remember things that had happened the night before. Some days I would say to myself – *I am not going to drink today* – but I became so anxious. I couldn't last longer than an hour or two and I would be out getting another bottle.

g)   *Physical changes – extreme mood swings, sleeping a lot more or less than usual and at different times, changes in energy level, weight loss or gain, unexpected or persistent coughs or sniffles, seeming unwell at certain times and better at other times, and pupils of eyes were seeming smaller or larger than usual.*

h)   *Psychological / Behavioural changes – secretiveness, paranoid, lying, stealing, financial unpredictability, changes in social group and activities. "Often addicts are the only ones who think their addiction is a secret. They believe the lies are hiding the secret, but those close to them have noticed they are drinking too much, abusing prescription drugs, gambling away necessary funds, overeating, purging, shopping, living in clutter etc. Addicts may know what others know but they continue to tell lies and continue to hurt only themselves."*

Lies, lies and more lies. That was my life I had to keep thinking of lies to keep my previous lie alive. It was hard to remember what lie you told and to whom. I lied about how much I was drinking to everyone. I became secretive. I would hide my bottles around the house. It was so embarrassing when my kids would find the empty bottles. My whole life was a lie.

i) *Blaming* – *"Placing blame for behaviour on others, on a situation is an old ploy of addicts that keeps them from taking responsibility for their choices." Addicts are rarely accountable for their own behaviour. They blame their parents, their upbringing, their relationship to continue to use. They never look at themselves.*

I blamed everyone and everything for my drinking. First, it was my parents and my alcoholic upbringing. Then, it was my two ex-husbands. Next, it was because I was a struggling single mother and then it was my countless destructive relationships. I blamed the guys I dated. I never looked at myself.

The only symptom that I did not relate to was the physical changes. I am sure if I had kept drinking, it would have eventually affected my physical appearance. It was difficult to realize that I had a problem. I was an alcoholic and I needed to change my life. If I kept on the path that I was on, I would not survive. I started to question – Why? What happened to me in my childhood? Did

I have a physical defect in my brain? None of my siblings had a problem with alcohol, why me? I was feeling a little anxious about where my alcoholism came from. The next chapter reviews some of the causes that may lead to alcoholism. Again, I tried to see which causes I could relate too.

Chapter 5

. . . .

Factors contributing to Alcoholism

Why does one become an addict? Are they born an addict? Does society play a role in addiction? According to *Unchain Your Brain: 10 Steps to Breaking the Addictions that Steal Your Life* by Daniel Amen and David Smith, there are certain biological, psychological, social and spiritual factors that have an effect on addiction. I looked at all the areas of my life. The past and the present and I was able to relate my addiction to some of these specific factors. It took the total responsibility and blame off of my shoulders. I was able to look at my addiction from different aspects. I could relate to some of these factors and it actual became quite apparent that I was destined to be an alcoholic from the time I was born. It helped me to stop beating myself up for the things that I had done when I was drinking. When I took myself outside of the disease, I was able to take a long look at why I ended up the way I did.

BIOLOGICAL FACTORS:

"Biological make-up and the health of your brain can either help you to make good judgements and decisions or poor judgements to giving in to temptation." It is important that an addict understands that they are born with an addictive brain. An awareness of this defect helps the addict to stop blaming themselves for their addiction. But use the information to learn about and overcome their addiction. The biological factors include brain function, genetics, physical health and the dietary issues underlying addiction.

a) *Brain function: Research shows that an addict's brain is wired differently than a non-addict. Once an addict has their drug of choice a trigger is turned on in their brain. Whether the trigger is constantly stimulated, is the addict's choice of using or not. Also, if your brain is not functioning properly and is not healthy, this can lead to addictive behaviour. When your brain is troubled, you are more likely to have trouble with addictions.*

b) *Genetics: If there is addiction in your family history, you have more of a chance to become an addict. "According to the National Institute on Drug Abuse, genetic factors account for 40 to 60% of a person's vulnerability to addiction." If the addiction begins when a person is a teenager, the addiction is caused 60% by genetics and 40% by the environment.*

c) *Medical Conditions and Medications: If your body isn't healthy, your brain can not be healthy and therefore the vulnerability to become an addict increases. "Chronic pain conditions such as fibromyalgia, cause changes in the brain and often lead to a dependence on pain killers and other unhealthy coping mechanisms. Prescription medications can affect brain function in a negative way and increase someone's odds for addiction. Low blood sugar is another serious condition that decreases brain activity and lowers a person's ability to say 'no' to unhealthy substances and behaviours. Hormonal imbalances which occur during PMS or menopause can also effect brain activity and leave a person more vulnerable to rely on addictive substances."*

d) *Poor Nutrition: "Eating healthy is an important aspect of living a healthy lifestyle and maintaining proper brain activity and function." If someone eats unhealthy and substitutes nutrition with alcohol or other substances lead to a dependency and ultimately an addiction. Also, some woman become obese, take diet pills, get addicted to the diet pills and ultimately start to drink because the diet pills suppress their appetite and they require that sugar from alcohol.*

e) *Lack of Exercise: "Little to lack of physical exercise negatively affects blood flow in the body." The low blood flow affects the brain activity negatively. Low brain activity lowers someone's self-control and therefore they become more vulnerable to becoming addicted to something.*

f) *Lack of Sleep: Getting less than 6 hours of sleep a night may have a negative effect on a person's brain activity and function. Lack of sleep can cause poor judgement in thinking and in self-control.*

Changes in physical health and appearance that indicate an addiction include: sudden increases or decreases in activity or energy level, weight loss or gain, a lack of personal hygiene, strange body odour, red watery glossy eyes, changes in sleeping patterns, feeling sick or overtired, and blacking out or forgetting what happened while under the influence.

PSYCHOLOGICAL FACTORS:

Your psychological make-up includes all of the past experiences that have shaped your thinking patterns and ultimately shaped your behaviours – good and bad. Negative psychological factors may influence a person to isolate and engage in unhealthy substances or behaviours. Some of the psychological factors are self-talk, any past emotional trauma, past successes and failures and your upbringing, self-image and outlook on life.

> a) *Self-Talk: Negative self-talk can keep an addict in the addiction. Negative thoughts attract negative circumstances and subsequently continued negative behaviour including addiction.*
>
> b) *Past Emotional Trauma: "Many people seek solace of past physical, emotional or sexual trauma through addictive behaviour. Having endured any form of trauma significantly increases the risk of substance abuse." In most cases, people who have suffered abuse often use alcohol, drugs, food or other unhealthy behaviours to suppress negative emotions.*
>
> c) *Upbringing: The way you were raised has a psychological effect on your well-being. If you were raised in a chaotic environment without love and affection may have long-lasting negative effects on your adult life. "These early hurts and negative experiences may lead one to turn to an addiction as adults in order to numb the lack of love felt as a child. On the other hand, having been raised in a perfectionist home and by very*

demanding parents may create enormous amounts of stress in someone's adult life."

d) *Self-Image / Outlook on Life: The way you think about yourself and the way you think about the outside world can have a tremendous risk of one becoming an addict. "People with negative self-image and low self-esteem are more inclined to engage in unhealthy behaviours" A person may feel like they aren't worth taking care of themselves. This lack of self-respect and negative thoughts also creates an attitude of a hopeless future. In order to suppress these negative thoughts about oneself and the outside world, a person may turn to unhealthy behaviours and substances to suppress these feelings.*

e) *Past Successes and Failures: If people have a negative view of their past and perceived failures, they are more likely to turn to substance abuse to deal with these negative thoughts. On the other hand, if someone had many successes in life and suffers from lack of success in the present, sometimes turn to addictive behaviours to numb the sadness with lack of satisfaction in themselves and life.*

f) *Dealing with Grief: Some are able to cope with the death of a loved one or when a significant break-up occurs, they are able to bounce back from this devastating event. Others are unable to deal with this loss and suppress their feelings. This suppression leads to a reliance on something to keep the hurt and loss in its place. A person tends to seek anything to keep these feelings suppressed and numbed through alcohol, drugs, sex or food.*

The most common psychological signs of addiction include mood swings, feelings of depression, irritability, anger, negative attitude, inability to focus, lack of motivation, loss of interest and denying or minimizing the consequences of using substances or engaging in the behaviour.

SOCIAL FACTORS:

It is important to look at the stresses in life including relationships, work, school and finances as to the cause leading one to addiction. There are many life events and stresses that can trigger the inclination to develop bad habits. The overwhelming responsibilities of daily living, cooking and taking care of children, financial difficulties, relationship troubles, and problems at work can lead one to rely on alternatives to cope with these social issues. Even daily stresses and anxiety can have an effect on one's brain chemistry which may lead to addictive behaviour. Some of these social factors include relationships, work and school, finances, and thrill-seeking behaviour.

a) *Relationships: Although relationships with your family, friends and significant others are very important to your health and well-being, they are much more difficult to develop in our technological society. Gone are the days of meeting in person, everything from work, school and even starting relationships are done via the cell phone or laptop. A lack of social connection causes negative changes in the brain. Many people with addictions avoid any sort of relationships. They tend to isolate and hide from interaction. This behaviour is damaging and can lead one to substances to substitute the feeling of loneliness. Since we are social beings, having social connections and relationships keeps are brains healthy and properly functioning. Isolation and lack of social connections directly impacts our sense of well-being and lack of t leads to depression, anger and addictive behaviour.*

b) *Work and School: Relationships with people at work and at school can make your life miserable. A demanding overwhelming job or having a job that you do not enjoy can have a negative effect on your well-being. Often, problems with other students at work can cause low self-esteem and low self-confidence. Many turn to substances to relieve this esteem issue. Also, children are so quickly diagnosed with learning disabilities and put on prescription drugs starting when they are very young. Prescription drugs such as Ritalin are very addictive especially when started at such a young age. Many college students also get addicted to prescription stimulants to help with concentration, studying and alertness but this addiction may continue once school is done.*

c) *Finances: Financial problems can create a tremendous amount of stress. Many addicts use their financial woes as a reason to use and this escape from their financial hardships temporarily alleviate the thoughts of their problems. Also, drug addicts and alcoholics spend a great deal amount of money on their drug of choice. People with addictions tend to miss more days of work and get fewer promotions which lower any potential in reaching a higher level of employment.*

d) *Thrill-seeking Behaviour: In today's society, simple events such as receiving a text message can cause a release of dopamine in the brain and creating an instant high. Playing video games and watching high intensity television shows also creates this same effect on the brain. All of this instant dopamine rushes are slowly wearing out our pleasure centers. This decrease creates depression and anxiety and ultimately an addiction to alcohol, drugs, internet gambling, pornography and compulsive shopping to restore the pleasure centers in our brains.*

Social signs and symptoms of an addiction include negative changes in work performance, calling in sick, showing up late, missing meetings, problems with co-workers, and negative changes in school performance, skipping classes, failing grades, withdrawal from family and friends and becoming anti-social.

SPIRITUAL FACTORS:

Spiritual health is very important to one's overall well-being. Mind, body and spirit are connected to optimal health and well-being. Due to our society's reliance on technology, we have lost our faith in religion and spirituality. In today's society, a high percentage of people are dealing with depression and anxiety. There is limited use of mediation, yoga and spiritual practices and as a result people turn to an option to achieve spiritual awakening through drugs and alcohol and other addictive behaviours. Some of these behaviours include: keeping secrets, cheating and extra marital affairs, deliberately hiding things and information from others, lying, stealing, breaking promises and making excuses for behaviours.

Understanding some of the theories of symptoms, signs and causes of addiction and alcoholism helped me to become accountable for my alcoholism. On the other hand, it helped me not to beat myself up. Alcoholism is a disease. It is not something we choose, it is something we are born with. But how do we overcome this unwanted affliction? The following chapters are what I did to get through and overcome this disease. Hopefully some of the suggestions will help you as well.

Chapter 6

Alcoholics Anonymous/Relapse

There are a number of anonymous groups which are used by millions to overcome their addictions. Based on the basics of Alcoholics Anonymous, throughout history other groups have erected – Narcotics Anonymous, Gamblers Anonymous, Sex Anonymous and groups for many other addictions. My personal experience was with Alcoholics Anonymous. I found it to be a very powerful tool to overcoming alcoholism. The first step to recovery is awareness and admitting being an alcoholic. It is a very humbling experience to come to the conclusion that my life had become unmanageable. The first three steps of Alcoholic Anonymous are the most difficult to finally admit and surrender my ego.

Step 1 – We admitted we were powerless over alcohol that our lives had become unmanageable.

"Under the lash of alcoholism, we are driven to A.A. and there we discover the fatal nature of our situation. Then, and only then, do we become as open-minded to conviction and as willing to listen as the dying

can be. We stand ready to do anything which will lift the merciless obsession from us." Twelve Steps and Twelve Traditions – page 24

This is the hardest step to admit and accept. No one wants to give up the fight and say – "Yes, I am alcoholic." When I joined AA seven years ago, I wasn't ready to say that I was an alcoholic. I remember George took me to a meeting. When it was my turn to introduce myself, I just said "Hi, I'm Frances." They almost kicked me out but George saved me and I was able to stay in the meeting. I thought that I had accepted this step – which my life was unmanageable and I was powerless over alcohol. But in December I slipped up and had a drink. My body refused the alcohol and I got incredibly sick. I spent the night in the bathroom and I had the spins. I had forgotten the severity of my hangovers. The next day at the A.A. meeting, I told the members that I had a relapse. It was at that moment that I accepted the fact that I was an alcoholic. It was an amazing uplifting experience. During the first six months of my sobriety I was still not one hundred percent sure that I truly was an alcoholic. That awareness is the first step in A.A. and in changing your life.

Step 2 – Came to believe that a Power greater than ourselves could restore us to sanity.

"Therefore, Step Two is the rallying point for all of us. Whether agnostic, atheist, or former believer, we can stand together on this step. True humility and an open mind can lead us to faith, and every A.A. meeting is an assurance that God will restore us to sanity if we rightly relate ourselves to Him." Twelve Steps and Twelve Traditions – page 33

When I think back to a year ago, my life was totally out of control. I never thought that I would ever be able to stop. The amount that I was drinking was ridiculous. I knew I was strong after going through all of the situations in my life. But to stop my drinking, I knew I couldn't do it on my own. I do not think that I, alone, conquered my alcoholism. I came to believe that a Higher Power something bigger than me intervened and restored my life to sanity.

Step 3 – Made a decision to turn our will and our lives over to the care of God as we understood Him.

"In all times of emotional disturbance or indecision, we can pause, ask for quiet, and in the stillness simply say: God grant me the serenity to accept the things I cannot change, courage to change the things I can, and wisdom to know the difference. Thy will, not mine, be done." Twelve Steps and Twelve Traditions – page 41

I grew up Catholic so initially I was skeptical about turning my will over to the care of God. The God that I was fearful of growing up wouldn't forgive my behaviour. There would have to be some sort of consequence for Him to forgive. The God that A.A. refers to is a God of our understanding. It can be anything that you can connect too. My personal Higher Power is the God-within me and in each and every human. It is the soul or the Holy Spirit that lives in my subconscious mind. It the source behind my intuition and it is the power that took my obsession with alcohol away.

"It's important that we share our experiences with other people. Your story will heal you and your story will heal somebody else. When you tell your story, you free yourself and give other people permission to acknowledge their own story." Iyanla Vanzant

Alcoholics Anonymous is a place where alcoholics share their stories with each other. It is a place where an alcoholic doesn't have to feel ashamed or embarrassed to tell the truth. The fellowship is like a family – no judgements, no alienation, no isolation and no loss of self-esteem or confidence. Although the spiritual side of Alcoholics Anonymous and the surrender to a High Power aids in eliminating alcohol addictions, I believe that some A.A. members believe that there still exists a duality between oneself and their Higher Power. One is separated from God. I believe that God exists inside each one of us. We are part of the Divine therefore duality does not exist. "We are all spiritual beings having a human experience." This awareness awakened the power within me to conquer my addiction. I try to go to five to six A.A. meetings a week. Where else can you get together with like-minded people sharing their concerns and feelings about the same addiction – alcoholism? A.A. is truly a place where I can be myself and it has been a blessing in my life. I am presently working on the remaining steps in the program. I repeatedly return to Step 1 when I get that crazy thought that I am a normal drinker. Staying sober each day is a lot of work psychologically, spiritually and physically. It is a battle worth fighting though because the benefits of a sober life greatly outweigh the benefits of an alcoholic life.

A person can work recovery to the best of their ability. There are many reasons why relapses occur. It could be a stressful life situation or the alcoholic feels confident that he can drink like a normal person. Whatever the reason, the most important thing is to pick up the pieces, admit your relapse, and let it go. There is no need for shame or guilt. By definition, *relapse is a temporary return to the problematic behaviour.* (Alternatives to Abstinence). According to statistics, a relapse most often occurs within the first month of recovery. After detox, I was so against having another drink. I hardly got any cravings. I started going to AA meetings about five to six times a week. The cravings really started to kick in after my first rehab. I was pretty confident after my 18 day treatment at Newport. I was discharged on July 26th. I had the cravings but was able to control them through the coping skills that I learned in treatment. At this time, I was also getting some therapy. The therapist recommended that I ask my doctor to put me on anti-depressants. She did two tests and concluded that I had high anxiety and mild depression.

Most alcoholics are diagnosed with some sort of anxiety and depression. I started on Cipralex 10 mg. They were increased to 20 mg within the first month. I was feeling pretty good and confident. I decided to have a couple of glasses of wine on my birthday. My tolerance had decreased so much. I felt the effect of the wine very quickly and more intense. I got very dizzy and ended up on the bathroom floor. I don't remember much from that night. My memory wasn't very clear. It was a horrible experience. After a few hours lying on the bathroom floor, I crawled into my bed. I think by three or four in the afternoon, I felt a little better. I tried to blame it on the combination of the wine and the anti-depressants. I was shocked that I was so sick. The experience made me realize that I was not able to drink anymore. It was a good lesson. I felt ashamed and guilty but I also knew that it wouldn't help beating myself up.

The next relapse I had was at Christmas time. It was the first Christmas alone and I was terrified to face it by myself. My mother is in an old age home and not in the best health. My sisters are all dealing with their lives and for the first time in years, we made no plans to get together for Christmas. My kids went to their dad's for dinner and my youngest son came over on Christmas day for a few hours. It was very depressing. I ended up drinking on December 30th. Again, I had two drinks and I ended up passed out on the couch. I didn't want to move. I knew I would have the spins if I tried to stand up. The guy I was with walked me downstairs to go to sleep. I threw up all over the mattress. I felt absolutely horrible. When I woke up the next morning, I knew I could not drink even a drop of alcohol. I was an alcoholic.

My life would quickly become unmanageable if I returned to that lifestyle. I felt very guilty and ashamed. I spoke about my relapse at AA and at my outpatient program group. Relapses are actually very helpful. My two relapses made me realize that I cannot drink. No matter how confident I am in my recovery, I know that I cannot drink. I made a commitment to myself that day to surrender my will and my cravings to my Higher Power.

The two most powerful lessons I learned and which was the hardest to get a handle of was:

1. that we as human beings are all part of the Divine, the Creator, and the Universe. We are spiritual beings having a human experience;

2. that we are the sole creators of our experiences through the Law of Attraction.

We are all spirits who came with a blueprint of what lessons we wanted to learn and what experiences we needed to have to learn them. Subconsciously or consciously through our thoughts and our words we created everything in our lives. It was difficult for me to grasp that idea. Why would I create the situation to be alone, or broke, or stricken with a disease? What lesson did I want to learn when I created my blueprint? It's so much easier to say that life happens and we have to adjust to it. Taking responsibility and accountability for your own life and its experiences is a very difficult thing to do.

I know I was out of control with my drinking but I couldn't stop. I created the accident on a subconscious level so that I would learn my lesson. I know in the past I have had experiences which I should have come to that conclusion – the numerous black-outs, the horrible hang-overs, and the severed friendships, but that wasn't enough. I needed something more serious to get the lesson through my head.

Since then, I know I created the reactions to the two relapses so that I would not want or crave to drink again. I still fight with cravings but now I have coping skills that help me get through them.

I'm not sure if I will ever be craving-free but I know with God's help I will fight through each and every one of them. I will not let this disease beat me down again. When you face challenges with the TRUTH that you created the situation and that you are a spirit having a human experience, the intensity of the challenge tends to lessen. You learn to treat the situation as a challenge and become aware of what the message that you are to acquire truly is. Anything that makes you feel good is your path. You are acting out your blueprint. Anything that feels bad means that you are off your path and you need to figure out the lesson in order to get back on the right track.

I was terrified to go to court… It was an absolute awful experience. The first five times that I had to go, I let me insecurity and fear take over. I placed my ego above the Divine within. As a result, I became extremely anxious. I remember crying uncontrollably and feeling sorry for myself. I played into my ego's pity party. I soon realized that I am not a victim. I created this situation so that I can learn from it. Also, my Higher Power, my will, knew that I was strong enough to handle it. Your inner self would not create more than you can physically and mentally handle. I looked at my strength and realized its power.

The next time I went to court, I was still full of insecurity and fear but I consciously looked around at the other people who sat around me. They were all experiencing the same thing as me. They had been arrested or charged and had the same insecurities and low self-worth as I did, I felt connected with them. There was no duality just a common bond. I then looked at the other side of the room where the lawyers and judge were. I realized that they too were connected to me and with everyone in the room.

All of us were living out our blueprint according to what we wanted to learn in this lifetime. It was a very calming experience. It didn't take away my fear but I was able to lessen my fear's intensity. Believe me; I have a few more court sessions to go to. I am not looking forward to them or the ultimate result of the trial but now I can approach the situation in a more conscious way. I control my fear and thought about it. Not the other way around.

Chapter 7
. . . .
My Seven Spiritual Lessons
for RECOVERY

After researching addictions and alcoholism and experiencing the trials and tribulations of recovery, I have chosen seven spiritual lessons from my Metaphysical Program through the University of Sedona that have helped me through this process. They are my guidelines for success and for continued sobriety.

Combing the knowledge and strength I gain through Alcoholics Anonymous with the spiritual TRUTHS I learned through my studies, I believe together they have saved me from returning to the Hell of my addiction. Once I realized the TRUTH that God, Higher Power, Ultimate Source, the Universe (whatever name you put on it) is within me and I surrendered my will, my thoughts and my problems to IT, my life began to run smoothly. By acknowledging that I had the power within me, there was no more need for any duality between me and my Higher Power. Believe me, it is a daily struggle to not give in to the anxiety and fear of the future and what is going to happen with my court case and my job, but surrendering it daily brings a sense of peace into my life for that day. I surrender and have complete trust and faith in my Higher Self. I know that the God-within would not give me more than I could handle.

When you combine mind, body and spirit, you will experience intuitive thoughts coming from your Higher Self. You will know that you are controlling your life and not being controlled by it. You will begin to feel less alone but in a partnership with your Higher Self. The shame and guilt of the past is gone, the worry and anxiety of the future doesn't exist, when you realize your Higher Self is within you and will guide you in the right direction. Then everyday can be lived to its fullest. Breathe in the cool air, bask in the sunshine, smell the freshly cut grass, watch the squirrels play with each other. This life is about fully experiencing each and every moment. Your Higher Power within will take care of the rest. Surrender to your Higher Power – and start to LIVE.

SEVEN SPIRITUAL LESSONS FOR RECOVERY SUCCESS

Lesson 1: Conscious Spiritual Self-Realization for Success

"The quickest way to rid oneself of negativity is to focus the mind on the TRUTH: that truth being SELF-TRUTH. When, in the midst of negativity we can remind our conscious mind of the TRUTH of WHOM and WHAT we really are, a peace, an understanding fill our being. In truth, our REALITY is GOD expressing through physical form and matter." *(Bachelor's Program – Lesson 2)*

When we do not accept who we truly are – divine – we tend to abuse ourselves. *God or Higher Power or the Divine or the Universe* is within. People still look for a God outside of themselves. They look towards Heaven when they really need to look inside at their soul and spirit. Raised Catholic the concept of a Power-within me or God-within me was very difficult to grasp. There is no duality – no God out there and you here. Difficult concept to understand but through meditation , it became a clearer. I began to think, if my Higher Power is within me – and I am part of the Divine – then when I was self-critical of myself, I was being self-critical to my Higher Power. That just didn't make sense to me. Talk about crazy thinking - this one day I was complaining to myself about the weight I gained on my butt. "I can't believe how big my butt is. I need to work out. I look awful," and then it hit me I am saying to God – "Your butt is big and you look awful." How could the ultimate Power, the Divine, the Universe, the source that created all things be concerned about a few extra pounds? I started to laugh thinking of how insane it was to comment and criticize myself. If we are all a part of the Divine, then criticizing yourself, you are actually criticizing God. It was a hard concept to understand but once I allowed myself to see the TRUTH in the matter, it was pretty funny.

I also began to think that I was putting my addiction above my Higher Power. I began to think that if I drank I was turning my back on God- within and I realized how selfish I was being. It was as if I was saying to my Higher Power – "I'm better than you." When you continue your addiction, you are turning your back on the truth and the Divine Universe. An addictive mind is selfish, an awakened mind is compassionate.

Lesson 2: Establishing Mystical Self-Direction

"Just as it easier for most people to take a tranquilizer, rather than to solve the cause of tension, so it is easier for most to let the opinions of others guide them, rather than to do their own thinking. The tranquilizer covers up what really should be done. In the same respect, as to direction in one's life, there is not a real solution or 'rising above' those things that keep a person from attaining happiness and success to a measure that would give one a true sense of fulfillment. The choice is yours. That is, to go along with the majority of society, living a life of quiet frustration, or to be guided by an inner wisdom to a fulfillment in life through the PRESENCE of the ALL-KNOWING MIND of GOD within you." (*Bachelor's Program Lesson 7*)

If you turn on the television, it is very rare that you won't see an alcohol commercial promoting youth, fun and happiness with drinking a certain brand. The media and the internet are covered with ads for alcohol, cigarettes and on many teenager social sites there are blogs and instagram pictures of marijuana and other substances. Peer pressure also plays a role in continuing an addiction. One must truly want to be free of living behind a mask and being the unique divine human that they are. It is a difficult task because once you decide on a new life one free of your addiction; you soon lose your old lifestyle including friends that you may have had for years. Many addicts get to this point when they are blatantly told by a doctor that if they continue on their addictive path that they will die. Awareness and self-honesty helps an addict realize that they must face their fate and step aside from the norm and the societal pressures of covering up problems and surrender to their Higher Power. They must have faith that their God-within will guide them to a drug-free life. One must listen to their inner voice also called intuition. This is how the God-within communicates. When an addict is high, their awareness and intuition are very low but when an addict stops using, the communication barrier is decreased and the God-within can guide them in the right direction. An addict's focus, inner strength and awareness are elevated and the truth of their divinity is more easily seen and experienced when sober and clean.

Lesson 3: Establishing Positive New Patterns in Your Life

"A pattern is more than a physical appearance. It is a manifestation of a psychic force active in one's life. Psychologically, we may speak about the effects of positive or negative patterns in the subconscious mind, but with psychic and spiritual wisdom, we can gain further insight as to how to handle such patterns. We will use psychic and spiritual energy and presence, respectively, to influence established mental patterns. We will use positive thought programming to plant seeds of new life experience in the mind. We will invoke the DIVINE PRESENCE of GOD-POWER in the unconditioned center of the mind, to act in removing unwanted patterns and for the establishment of positive new patterns." Bachelor's Program – Lesson 13

An addiction is a negative pattern in the brain chemistry. Once an addict has stopped the drug of choice, it takes approximately one year for new positive patterns to be established in the brain. That is why the first year of sobriety is so critical to learn behaviours that help with this process. I have used the following techniques to aid in developing my new patterns. When I have a craving or I become anxious which is a pretty common withdrawal symptom with alcoholics, I take a few moments to practice the breathing exercises. I soon become calm and at peace. Incense and candle burning create a positive psychic energy atmosphere in my house. I believe surrounding oneself in white light daily and especially in slippery situations and places helps with the cravings. These physical tasks as well as the affirmations listed in the lesson have helped with my recovery and sub sequentially with my new developing sober healthy brain patterning and chemistry. It is very important that an addict in recovery to change their old activity patterns and create new patterns. This stimulates the brain and also provides different experiences to fill up the pleasure part of the brain that has been emptied once the drug of choice is eliminated from the body.

Lesson 4: Motivation

"GET UP AND GET GOING WITH GOD – not with yourself! Let God 'DO' not you. Give God the credit, not yourself. Believe that God is the one doing, not you!" Bachelor's Program – Lesson 31

The factor that is limiting an addict's motivation is the thought that they are all alone to make these drastic changes in their lives in order to recovery. Being a member of a fellowship such as AA or NA, provide camaraderie among fellow addicts, there is still the element of individuality when facing life. The most rewarding aspect in recovery is when you finally surrender your will over to God and put the onus on the future and the outcome onto Him. God is within each one of us. We are never alone. When we are practicing our addiction, God does not exist. If He does, it is in a duality sense and usually called upon in desperation. But in recovery, God becomes an inner presence and the feeling of isolation and loneliness no longer exists. God is doing for you, what you cannot do for yourself. Once you surrender, you are given a hidden power that motivates you to do healthy positive things even when you sometimes do not feel the energy or the reason for doing it. Do not beat yourself up if you lack motivation in your daily lives. I was having a rough day and I had a really strong craving. I was on my way to the liquor store when I passed the Humane Society. It was a beautiful day. I pulled in and I went to look at the dogs. I fell in love with this beautiful *chug*. After spending a few hours with the dog, I adopted her the next day. My big black lab *Prince* wasn't happy at first but now the three of us are best friends. If I didn.t have these two, some days I would never get out of bed.

Lesson 5: Overcoming

"Overcoming is the acceptance that God is the highest essence of your self-identity, and the action that follows such an acceptance.

If you have been experiencing a miserable time in your attempt to overcome your problems, obviously, something must change. Such a change is not one that will take place outside of yourself; that change will have to be made inside yourself." Bachelor's Program – Lesson 33

The biggest moment in an addict's life is when they finally accept their addiction and they are able to admit – "I am an addict." With some addicts this process happens quickly, but with others the process takes years and years and most often after they have hit rock bottom or lost everything. Personally, my bottom and my realization that I was an alcoholic came following a car accident. I had a van full of students and I was arrested for impaired driving in front of them. It was humiliating. I spent the night in jail. The media jumped on the bandwagon quickly – "Local teacher charged with impaired driving." After years of convincing myself that I was a 'normal' drinker, God woke me up that day. I gave up the fight and I admitted that I had an addiction. The work of recovery is then transferred from blaming others on the outside to finally looking within you and becoming accountable.

> *"Let the Presence of God, within you, be your foundation for self-confidence. Think of the word 'self' as in 'self-confidence' as a self that is one with God, a God-self. So, instead of feeling a lack of self-confidence, begin feeling the fullness of your God-self-confidence."*

This sentence changed the way I viewed myself and my addiction. I realized that when I lacked self-confidence, I was actually turning my back on my Higher Power. When I chose to drink, I was disrespecting my God-within. This one thought helped change my life. Once I realized that I was one with my God-self, my selfish thoughts disappeared and I no longer craved negative thoughts about myself and I no longer craved a substance that harmed by body which held my Higher Power.

Lesson 6: Moderation

"Moderation…the person who chooses to live within moderation will seldom be faced with extreme situations of his own majesty. Without making an issue of it to anyone but yourself, have a oneness of identity with God; and then continue life, neither craving and running after any whim or fancy of enjoyment that may come along, nor withdrawing either." (Bachelor's Program – Lesson 42)

This lesson was the most influential on my recovery to date. Recovery is an individual process. It requires self-discipline, self-worth, lots of faith and commitment to the God-within. It is so important to have a connection with your Higher Power within. It is important to not give into cravings. It is also important to stay connected to the outside world and not become withdrawn and isolated which may return to relapse. Moderation, moderation, moderation – an addict tends to become addicted to everything because of their addictive personality. Once the drug of choice is taken away, it is important that the addict does not substitute another addiction for the one that they had just given up. An addict will refrain from drinking alcohol but may get very addicted to exercise and exercise to the extreme. Moderation is the key to a successful recovery. To fully accept moderation, an addict must surrender completely to their Higher Power for guidance from the Divine within. This is the hardest part of an addict's recovery.

Lesson 7: Establishing and Accomplishing Your Goals

"To succeed in life in any area, certain goals must be

established. Without goals the mind tends to wander and become distracted from accomplishing anything in life. Without a sense of accomplishment life can seem lifeless and meaningless. If you yourself are to truly find your real goals and accomplish them, you have to turn WITHIN. Within the higher, spiritual, and God region of your mind the TRUE GOALS for you in life abide. Once you find them you will also find additional power to accomplish them." Bachelor's Program – Lesson 48

Setting small goals for yourself every day and accomplishing them is a great way to build self-esteem and confidence. Slowly build up your individual goals daily. The sense of accomplishment achieved makes life more positive and meaningful. We are all here for a reason. If you are struggling to find happiness in your work or home life then there is something missing. When you are on your right path and you are following your God-within, you are able to find happiness in everything in your life. I am still trying to figure out my purpose in life. I consciously observe what things make me happy and what things cause my stomach to knot. I try to listen to my intuition. I now know that it is my Higher Self trying to tell me what path is right and wrong.

Chapter 8
Daily Guidelines To Keeping Sober

Staying sober is a daily struggle. I still have cravings and I still feel myself wanting to fall back into that old lifestyle. I know it is just my addictive mind trying to convince me to pick up that first drink. This daily guideline has helped me maintain my sobriety and helps me build a stronger connection with my Higher Self.

a) **Meditate Daily** – meditation creates a connection to your Higher Power. This is also a time that you can receive messages from God within. It is time for your ego to 'shut up' and listen. I use self-guided meditations in the morning and at night. Caroline Myss and Kelly Howell are my favourites.

b) **Keep Your Body Clean** – A body that is clean gives off better vibrations. A positive pleasant vibration which radiates from a clean body attracts more pleasant things into your life. I have tried to keep good hygiene and as well as a healthy diet. We are spiritual beings using this physical body to learn and experience life. Our bodies are our temple and should be treated that way. Definitely our temples do not function well when they are abused with addictive substances. This is a difficult commitment at first. Start slowly everyday by doing stretches, walking and yoga. I recently started doing yoga and I absolutely love it. It combines spirituality with the strength of the body. I used to work out quite a bit with weights or on different machines. The one gym I went to had small televisions on each machine. As I was working out, I could catch up on my soap opera. Not very spiritual. But yoga helps you exercise your body, mind and spirit. I just throw on my sweatpants and a tank top and my living room acts as a yoga studio for a half hour or so.

c) **Dedicate Each Day to God and The Universe** – It is important to surrender your will over to your Higher Power and to acknowledge and be grateful each day to God-within for another day of sobriety and all of the blessings in your life. The fact that you wake up in the morning without feeling awful is a blessing! I think back to those mornings after a night of drinking. So many times I wished I wasn't able to wake up. I am grateful every day that I do not have a hangover. I am grateful that I am awake early. I surrender all of my problems to my Higher Power. It is such a relaxing and calming feeling when you live life without worry. My Higher Power will guide me, direct me and intuitively lead me down the right path. The minute something feels a little weird in my gut, I know it's not on my path. This took me so long to finally let go. I would continue on with a situation even though my gut and now I know my Higher Power was against it. My marriages are great examples of this. I intuitively felt that getting married wasn't the right answer but I went through with both of them.

d) **Nullify Negative Thoughts and Negative Spoken Words** – It is a conscious effort to become aware of negative thoughts and try to stop them before they fix themselves in your subconscious mind and to fester. With clarity which abstinence brings to the recovering addict, it is easier to become aware of negative thoughts and as a result it makes it easier to change negative thoughts to positive thoughts. Remember that they are just thoughts. They have no power or control over you unless you give them that power.

e) **Read Inspirational Literature** – As little as five minutes a day of reading inspirational literature can raise your vibrational level throughout the day. Fellowships such as Narcotics Anonymous and Alcohol Anonymous have daily reflection books which are based on the 12-step program. Also, the basics text of both NA and AA provide a detailed description of each step and stories of addicts which had eventually succeeded in their recovery. I started this journey many years ago when I picked up *The Celestine Prophecy*. I didn't know I was on a journey but the principles outlines in the book made me ponder my life and my thoughts. From there I read *The Way of the Peaceful Warrior, The Road Less Travelled, and You Can Heal Your Life."* All three are very powerful and eye-opening books. Next I read all of the *Conversation with God* books. I went to a psychic who told me I needed to read *Excuse Me Your Life Is Waiting* by Lynn Grabhorn. I gravitated toward her books because she was an ex-alcoholic. Her book *Beyond the Twelfth Step* had an impact on me. I was able to relate with the void feeling that may still exist even after you have joined AA. Lately I have been reading *Esther and Jerry Hicks* books and watching their seminars on You-tube. They clearly explain the law of attraction and learning to manifest your desires.

f) **Keep Peace with Yourself and Your Environment–** An addict's life is filled with guilt and shame over their behaviour and their addiction, itself. The goal of recovery is to surrender this guilt and shame to the God-within, and fill your soul with peace and harmony. To hang onto that guilt and shame will also lead to a relapse. It is very important to 'Let Go and Let God' and creates a sense of peace in one's life.

It is very important to create a positive and calm home environment. I recently took down old pictures and paintings and hung up spiritual wall hangings and posters. Just that act alone created a more peaceful environment. I smudged my house with white sage to get rid of the negative energy attached to the house. We create a negative vibration in our homes when we have negative thoughts, or negative things happen there, or fighting etc. Burn a white sage stick and walk around the house asking for the negativity to leave the house. It is important to smudge clothing or certain rooms that holds memories of the past. Then you use sweet grass either incense stick or bundle and you ask for positive energy to enter your house. You trace the steps that you did with the white sage but this time you wave the smoke in a clock wise circle with your hand and ask for positive energy. This is also a great way to get rid of any bad spirits or spirits in general that you wish to leave your house.

Incense is another way to create positive energy in your home environment. It purifies and cleanses the psychic air of negative thought forms and vibrations. This quote is on the back of my favourite incense and it makes so much sense.

The Virtues of Incense – (from a 16th century Japanese Manuscript) it brings communication with the transcendent. It purifies mind and body. It removes uncleanliness. It keeps you alert. It can be a companion in the midst of solitude. In the midst of busy affairs, it brings a moment of peace. When it is plentiful, one never tired of it. When there is little, one is satisfied. Used every day, it does no harm.

My favourite incense is sweet grass and sandalwood but there are so many others that you can choose from. It brings a sense of peace and serenity into your home.

g) **Associate with Evolved People / Attend Metaphysical Groups** – Slippery people and places will disappear from an addict's life once recovery is in process. By joining a recovery group, you begin to attract similar people into your life. Surrendering to God will also create a spiritual mindset that you will want to be around people that are on the same spiritual level. In both of the treatment centers that I attended, they taught various metaphysical and spiritual practices to include in your daily regime. Once you are in this vibration, it is very difficult to return to the addictive world. Your eyes are open to the power of the universe and the God-within and the positive vibrations you send out will only attract equal vibrational souls to enter your atmosphere. Go to meetings and be around like-minded people.

h) **<u>Think Positively</u>** – It is very important that an addict begins to change their negative views to positive ones. Positive thoughts will vibrate positively and will attract positive experiences people and circumstances to you. You create your own reality through your thoughts. Always be aware of what you are thinking. What you think about, you will create – the Universe doesn't judge good or bad, it just responds to your thoughts. It is not only thinking positively, it is becoming aware of your negative thought and releasing those thoughts. It is not important to think positively but you must think positively. When you vibrate in a positive way, the universe will return positive situations to you. If you try to think positive but deep down you are negative about something. The universe picks up on your underlying feeling. Therefore the underlying negative attitude will be what the universe attracts too.

The Universal Law of Attraction will always create experiences in your life which match the deeply held beliefs that you hold in your subconscious mind. This goes for positive beliefs, as well as for negative beliefs. If you don't use spiritual healing techniques to get rid of the negative beliefs permanently, then the law will eventually bring you conditions which match your negative beliefs.

It's best to never stop saying prayers for healing. They allow you to continue to experience the good that you have now, and they can also help you to attract even more good in your life. Spiritual Awakenings.

i) **Remember Daily Who You Are** – It is important to remember the TRUTH daily. We are all part of the Divine and that God lives within each of us.

I was having a very difficult forgiving myself for the accident and placing the students as well as my daughter at risk. I hid from the world and became extremely introverted. I didn`t go to the local grocery store and I put my hood over my head when I walked my dogs. No matter how I tried to talk myself into not feeling embarrassed and shame, nothing helped. I went to a meeting and I was distant and distraught. It was a closed meeting and one of topics was forgiveness (coincidentally). I mentioned that I couldn`t get over the shame and embarrassment of the accident. I couldn`t forgive myself. An older gentleman wrote something on a piece of paper and handed it to me. ``If you truly believe that GOD has forgiven you (and he has), who are you to take that back. Are you more powerful then GOD? Accept his forgiveness! `` This hit me like a ton of bricks. If GOD forgave me who am I to hang onto the guilt and shame. I was really worried about what other people would say about me. I was so afraid to run into anyone and I stayed in my house for quite a long time. Another very wise friend said to me, ``the people that say something to you are really saying it to themselves. Maybe they deep down know that they have a drinking problem and by judging you, it helps them to hide their own problems. ``

Both of those pieces of advice helped me immensely but it was still very difficult for me to readjust back into society. I still have days when I am outside of my body looking in on this poor woman who is living my life. I sometimes forget that I was arrested and spent time in detox and rehabs. My friend from rehab and I were invited to party for another friend that we had met in rehab. He was celebrating three months clean and his family had asked us to come for the celebration. I was excited for my friend and I was looking forward to going but then it occurred to me – we are his friends from rehab. All the stigmas and stereotypes of ``addicts in rehabs`` came to me and I was too ashamed to go. We do not only face our own demons and battles trying to cage the disease, we will also be judged unjustly by society.

Chapter 9
My Steps and Affirmations To Recovery

This is a list of ten facts that I repeat daily as well as the affirmation for each. I also listed the characteristic that each step and affirmation illustrate. I surround myself with as much positivity as I can every day. Some days it is a chore. I wake up full of self-pity and completely in self-pity mode. On these days, it takes me a little longer to get motivated. By the time I finish my coffee and the dogs have licked my entire face, I am out of my victim role. I thank God for my life and for people around me. I thank HIM for the earth, nature and the beautiful animals. I then start with the following:

1. I am an alcoholic.   **ACCEPTANCE**

    Affirmation - I take accountability and responsibility
    for my sobriety and recovery.

2. I release the past. I live in the Now. I have no control over the
    future   **COURAGE**

Affirmation – I am no longer a victim of my past.

Serenity Prayer

God, grant me the serenity to accept the things I cannot change, the courage to change the things I can and the wisdom to know the difference.

3. I think positive thoughts. I ignore negative thoughts. **BELIEVE**

Affirmation – I release self-pity and self-defeating thoughts.

4. I am never alone. My Higher Power guides me along the right path. **FAITH**

Affirmation – I listen to my intuition. I am Divinely guided.

5. People that judge me, are insecure in their own lives. **NON JUDGEMENTAL**

Affirmation – I do not take anything personally that people say or do.

6. I am Divine. **LOVE**

Affirmation – I love, accept and approve of myself.

7. I am not my behaviour **COMPASSION**

Affirmation - I am a spiritual being having a human experience. I create my own reality and every situation has a lesson to be learned.

8. I overcome all obstacles on my road to recovery. **STRENGTH**

Affirmation – I am improving each day. I am more powerful than I know. I have unlimited potential.

9. I see the world with clarity and awareness. I make appropriate boundaries in my life. **HOPE**

   Affirmation – My God-within is stronger than any insecurity, anxiety and obstacle that comes in my path.

10. The hardships and troubles I face in my life are there for me to learn a lesson. **PERSERVERENCE**

    Affirmation – I move closer to the Divine each day. I will never be given more than I can handle.

Life is not as complicated and serious as we make it. We are here to have the experiences that we planned as spiritual beings. Each moment is here to learn and grow closer to the Source or God. The struggles and challenges we are confronted with, are subconsciously created in our minds so that we can learn the right lesson. Life is fun and should not be complicated with silly insecurity and useless emotion. The universe will keep creating the same situation until you learn the lesson and change your attitude and behaviour. Work on these affirmations daily and you will soon see changes in your life.

Review this poem when you are overcome with emotion in any situation.

WHY COMPLICATE LIFE?

Missing somebody?.......................call

Wanna meet up?.....................................invite

Wanna be understood?..........................explain

Have questions?..ask

Don't like something?............................say it

Like something?.....................................state it

Want something.........................ask for it

Love someone............................tell it

WE JUST HAVE ONE LIFE, KEEP IT SIMPLE! *Gregg Braden*

INSPIRATIONAL QUOTES

These are inspirational quotes that I read and meditate on daily. I hope they will help you on your road to sobriety.

Did you know the people that are the strongest are usually the most sensitive? Did you know the people who exhibit the most kindness are the first to get mistreated? Did you know the one who takes care of others all the time are usually the ones who need it the most? Did you know the 3 hardest things to say are I love you, I'm sorry, and Help me? Sometimes just because a person looks happy, you have to look past their smile and see how much pain they may be in. -Unknown

The willingness to share does not make one charitable; it makes one free. ~ Robert Brault

At the core of your being, there is love. Love is your spiritual identity. Every experience, every encounter, every lesson learned is life's way of training you to be a greater expression of love. Iyanla Vanzant

Things in this universe do not just happen, they are made to happen; either deliberately or unknowingly by our own actions. And taking this matter to a higher realm we can draw the conclusion that if energies can be put in motion, then they can also be directed.

Spiritual Awakenings

Take all your experiences and become empowered by them. You can't change them, but you can discover something of value in them. When you do, you'll be able to extend forgiveness to yourself and others. You won't carry the barriers and the weights of the past—you'll be free.

Unknown

You are good enough, smart enough, beautiful enough, strong enough. Believe it and stop letting insecurity run your life.

Thema Davis

Don't stoop to lower levels of behavior if others around you are. The only person you can control is yourself, not others. Choose integrity, love and wisdom and whoever doesn't get it, that is their problem, not yours. Don't give up the best of who you are to battle those who don't care... Don't give it up for anyone. Just stay centered.

Unknown

Don't carry your mistakes around with you. Instead, place them under your feet and use them as stepping stones!

Unknown

Worry is the direct descendant of the need to be in control. We cannot see everything. We do not know everything. It's impossible for us to control everything. Keep in mind that the process of life is a spiritual one, governed by invisible, intangible spiritual laws and principles.   Unknown

There are no mistakes, no coincidences. All events are blessings given to us to learn from.
Elisabeth Kubler-Ross

Appreciation and self-love are the most important tools that you could ever nurture. Appreciation of others, and the appreciation of yourself is the closest vibrational match to your Source Energy of anything that we've ever witnessed anywhere in the Universe. –
Jerry and Esther Hicks - Abraham

What matters is to live in the present, live now, for every moment is now. It is your thoughts and acts of the moment that create your future. The outline of your future path already exists, for you created its pattern by your past.
Unknown

The spiritual life is a call to action. Action without any selfish attachment to the results.
Eknath Easwar

When your deepest sadness is welcomed and fully felt, it can empty out your entire basement of horrors. All the incomplete feelings you've had in your life of being abandoned, betrayed, lonely, lost, or isolated can come flooding through. By opening up to your emotional basement you bring the light of awareness into the darkness.
Spiritual Awakenings

The truth is that our finest moments are most likely to occur when we are feeling deeply uncomfortable, unhappy, or unfulfilled. For it is only in such moments, propelled by our discomfort, that we are likely to step out of our ruts and start searching for different ways or truer answers

M. Scott Peck

This final lesson is the basis for an addict's recovery plan. I recently was in Homewood Rehabilitation and I was taught the importance of a disciplined scheduled daily routine. It is very important that an addict becomes accountable for their behaviours. If sobriety is to be successful, the addict must plan reachable goals (at first), must prepare a detailed do-able daily schedule and must be disciplined to follow the schedule thoroughly. The first few months of recovery are so important to establish routine and a schedule. During recovery, the addict must turn to his/her Higher Power for divine guidance of what are appropriate goals. Once the connection is made, the recovering addict must ask for help and guidance daily from the power within. If the goals are God-directed, then additional power will be given for the goals to be accomplished.

I believe that understanding the basis of an addiction from all aspects – biological, psychological, social and spiritual then pursuing recovery avenues such as AA, NA, counselling and medication but also developing an understanding of the TRUTH is the formula to finally caging the beast of addiction. Without the final step which is acceptance of the Universal Mind within oneself, a void and a feeling of emptiness will remain. Leaving that stone unturned for an addict can lead back to the addiction for fulfillment of this void. The void needs to be filled with the TRUTH.

The final step or the thirteenth step of recovery, in my opinion, is to surrender completely to the God-Within oneself and to have faith and confidence in His power.

The following quote from Kelly Howell – *The Universal Mind*. summarizes the TRUTH.

I will discover that the Secret Power within me that can help me do anything and become anything. I am one with the Universal Mind and I know this Mind is perfect and I may rely on it for guidance in all of my affairs. Inside of me is a place of confidence, quietness and security; a place where all things are known and understood. This is the Universal Mind – God, of which I am a part of, and which responds to me when I ask. This Universal Mind knows the answers to all of my problems and even now the answers are speeding its way to me. I needn't struggle for them, I needn't worry. When the time comes, the answers will be there. I give my problems to the great mind of God to the source of all creation. I let go of them confident that the correct answers will return to me when needed. Through the great Law of Attraction, everything I need for my worth and fulfillment comes to me. I have Divine Intelligence all around me. The Intelligence that created all things is in me and all around me.

The only true happiness, prosperity, peace, harmony, fulfillment and self-worth are found within yourself. Trying to find any of these outside of your self will surely fail. Once, I accepted who I truly was – a part of the Divine – I realized that I was never alone. My search for happiness and serenity brought me to the amazing realization that I am a part of God. This thought has made me overcome my addiction. It has finally given the peace and tranquility that I have been searching for my entire life. It's within each and every one of us and I am grateful and blessed that I have been chosen for this experience. My goal in life is to help others find the Truth and overcome their own demons and addictions. When I help others, I am helping myself by strengthening my connection to my Higher Power.

This is the first time in my life that I am single and I have never been happier. I would have never thought my life would change so much in a year. I have clarity and self-esteem. I am stronger than I ever thought I could be. I have a few challenges ahead of me. As long as I surrender the challenge and the outcome to my God-within, I will be guided along the right path. I will live *one day at a time* and have gratitude for being given a second chance. The world is a marvelous and amazing place to discover and explore. I am free. I am no longer imprisoned. I finally love myself. Life is better SOBER!

Bibliography

Books:

Amen, Dr. Daniel and Dr. David Smith, Unchain Your Brain – 10 Steps to Breaking the Addictions that Steal Your Life, MindWorks Press, 2010

Alcoholics Anonymous, Fourth Edition, Alcoholics Anonymous World Services Inc., New York City, 2001.

A Day at a Time – Daily Reflections for Recovering People, Hazelden, Center City, Minnesota 1989.

Gass, Justin T. Ph.D. "Understanding Drugs – Alcohol". Chelsea House Books, Infobase Publishing, New York, NY 2010.

Just for Today – Narcotics Anonymous World Services Inc., Van Nuys, California, 1992.

Living Sober, Alcoholics Anonymous World Services Inc., New York City, 2001.

Marks, Isaac. "Behavioural (Non-Chemical) Addictions." British Journal of Addiction 1990 85:1389 – 1394. 24 Jul 2008.

Masters, Paul Leon, 1989 Masters Degree Level Lesson: Volume 1. Burbank, CA. Burbank Printing Inc.

Twelve Steps and Twelve Traditions, Alcoholics Anonymous World Services Inc., New York City, 2009.

Websites:

Howell, Kelly, "The Universal Mind" 1998-2001

http://www.youtube.com/watch?v=tW4nyzXPDbE

http://www.kleantreatmentcenter.com/what-does-an-addict-look-like

http://www.seansabourin.com/what-does-an-addict-look-like

http://www.sharecare.com/question/addiction-takes-over-your-life

http://www.AmenClinics.com

www.spiritualawakenings.com

Songs:

The Broken Lyre – *Never Really Did*, 2012